THE WHEELER-DEALER

THE WHEELER-DEALER

By

Joseph Francis Panicello

North Hills Publishers
Northridge, CA
(818) 894-6729
Supported by The American Fiction Society
Other Books by Author
The Great Sicilian Norseman
Vindicated
Brian's Comet
A Man Of Destiny
How To Be A Successful Electronic Design Manager
Electronic Company Management

Printed in the United States of America, April 18, 2006

ISBN 1-58500-745-5

About the Book

The Wheeler-Dealer is the story of a man who came out of the streets of New York during the great depression where prohibition, gambling, loose women, and Speak-Easies were a way of life. The man was known as William "Bismarck" Jones. To survive in those poor days, a man had to use whatever means was available to him to support himself. Bismarck took the gambling route. When this became boring to him he upgraded himself into the confidence racket and fraud. He was very successful in all his endeavors, whether it be in sports or cards, he would always use his practiced skills to win a scam.

Bismarck was not born bad. It was a way of life at that time among his generation, so Bismarck became a pool shark. When no one would challenge him in New York any longer he tried other forms of gambling. He graduated to the confidence racket and eventually began stealing. He was not a bad man, he thought. When Bismarck embezzled money from a mark he wouldn't intentionally drive that person into bankruptcy. He would always leave the pigeon with enough assets to recoup himself. His greatest enjoyment was the challenge of the Con game and the thrill of victory.

Bismarck's only weakness was the opposite sex, He had a tendency to fall in love with his young female victims. This indulgent is considered tabu in the confidence racket. He did, however, fall in love with an Italian Countess whose father was one of his marks. This affair was almost his downfall.

Bismarck's main enemy was a Mr. Nichols who lost $100,000 in a golf game to Bismarck under a devious manner. Mr. Nichols became obsessed over his loss and decided to get even with Bismarck in a double sting operation employing the help of many of the people that Bismarck had fleeced. He was almost successful but Bismarck was too cunning.

The worst crime that Bismarck committed was to steal 5 million dollars worth of cocaine from the Mafia. The Mafia chief was enraged by this and was relentless in his effort to get his property back and to destroy Bismarck. This caused Bismarck to go on the run and he finally moved to England where he thought he would be safe. This distance did not stop the Mafia and attacked him in England.

When World War II began, Bismarck was afraid he would be drafted into the U.S. Army and become a lowly infantryman so he joined the Canadian Air Force. He bribed a key Canadian General into giving him a cushy job and to guarantee him that he would never have to fight in the war. It turned out, by accident, that this was not possible and Bismarck found himself right in the middle of it all. He had no interest in the war at all. He didn't care who won. He only cared about himself. His money was secure in other countries so why should he put his life on the line? In spite of his reluctance to fight he was forced into action and, because of some bizarre circumstances, he even became a hero.

The Monte Carlo Incident

His name is William "Bismarck" Jones. He's a confidence man, a hustler, and a highly successful gambler. He has the reputation of being the ultimate wheeler-dealer who is always on the lookout for easy pray. Not only was he able to swindle fortunes out of men with his refined manner and practiced maneuvers he had a special attraction about him that lured most women into becoming his victim. Some of his peers were fascinated with his talents and even honored him as the greatest of all Con men. Women romanticized over him and adored him as though he was a popular movie star. He was definitely an incredible swindler.

It was in the year of 1931 when Jones, at the age of 28, was at the peak of his so called devious career and was nicknamed "Bismarck" by a German rivalry, Karl Miller, while gambling in Monte Carlo on the French Riviera. Miller became captivated with the way William Jones handled himself as he watched him manipulate a deck of playing cards in a special poker game in a hotel suite entertaining several European aristocrats. The American version of poker was not played in European casinos at that time and had to be played in private parties. The French version was called poque and was slightly different. Many Europeans were fascinated with American poker and were willing to bet large sums in this unique card game. Jones was aware of their passion for the game and made himself readily available to fulfill their appetites and, of course, take their money. At these games Jones was always dressed in an expensive tuxedo looking rather distinguished and affluent. He knew these aristocrats wouldn't associate with anyone other than their own kind. He had to appear to be one of them.

The hotel room was very large with expensive French furniture. There were two tables in the room each illuminated by a chandelier directly above. The walls were decorated with large paintings depicting the Renaissance period and on the back wall there was a portrait of the late Prince of Monaco. Two waiters were busy providing food and drinks to the players. In no time the room became filled with cigar and cigarette smoke. In this one particular game Miller was watching Jones on the sideline as he operated and exploited these celebrities by taking them to the cleaners. By the late morning hours Jones was winning an enormous sum, over one hundred thousand equivalent American dollars. By this time the dignitaries decided they had enough and decided to quit for the day. After the game was over Jones cashed in his chips and was about to depart when Miller approached him and casually introduced himself.

"Mr. Jones. My name is Karl Miller. I was watching you playing poker just now, and I must say you are the best manipulating card player that I have ever seen." Miller had a distinct German accent. His remark, however, offended Jones.

"What are you insinuating, sir?"

"I'm not insinuating anything, Mr. Jones. I was merely expressing my opinion on how cunning you are at your play. You are marvelous. Outstanding, I must say. You remind me of the great Bismarck, the once powerful chancellor of Germany. You see, Otto von Bismarck was a conniver like yourself and a great manipulator in government strategy. He was a cunning chancellor, a master of diplomatic intrigue and used these talents to unify Germany."

Miller had a sarcastic smile on his face that irritated Jones. Unknown to Jones, Miller had this territory under his control for many years, even during World War I. He didn't particularly like any strangers horning in on him. Jones could sense that he was being prodded into an unnecessary confrontation, and tried to avoid an incident by walking away.

"Come, Mr. Bismarck. Don't you think you should share some of your winnings with me and avoid the authorities."

Jones knew he was being roped into a battle but even he had his limits. He looked directly into Miller's eyes with fire in his own and said, "Are you saying, sir, that I am a cheat? If so, I demand satisfaction."

"You shall have it, Mr. Jones. Name the time, the place and you may even choose the weapons." Miller still had that cynical smile on his face. He knew he had the edge being an accomplished swordsman himself and a superb marksman with the pistol. He purposely coerced Jones into this dual and knew it would be the easiest and fastest way to eliminate a potential rival. He had used this approach before to accomplished the same results. By killing off his competitors it would give him absolute assurance that they would never return again thus leaving the field open only to himself. Warnings didn't always work in these circumstances.

Miller was a tall man, about six foot four and weighed close to two hundred and forty pounds. He had blond hair that was cut very short on top and was shaved along the sides. It made him look even fiercer. He had a scar on his left cheek that came from a previous dual. His looks alone was enough to cause many a man to back down, but not Jones. He knew his own capabilities.

Jones didn't want to dual in the daylight that very morning so he selected that evening for the dual and in a field overlooking the ocean. He selected 22 caliber pistols. Miller could only grin at his selection knowing full well that he would have the advantage. What Miller didn't know, however, was that Jones used to hustle bets in Montana and Wyoming, challenging all those western cowboys in pistol contests. Jones was actually a trick-shot artist and could shoot a pistol or a rifle at thirty yards backwards over his shoulder looking into a mirror. He was once asked to join the late Wild Bill Coty's wild west show as their trick-shot artist with the aging Anne Oakly. Jones couldn't handle being tied down to one job like that. Shooting was just another one of his many talents that he used to hustle money. But his hustling was not just for the money, it was for the thrill of the victory which was much more exciting to him. He thrived on competition.

Jones, however, never left any confrontation up to chance. He would always take the necessary precautions to insure his survival. He chose 22 caliber pistols because they are not as deadly as the more powerful 45 or 38 caliber weapons. To be killed with a 22 pistol a shot had to be accurate and had to hit a vital part of the body. To guarantee his safety further, he wore a specially made vest that was not completely bullet proof but could be a deterrent against a 22 caliber slug. The vest was made of the same fabric that his suit was made of and would be undetected by the judge when he was being examined. No armor or protective apparel are allowed in a dual.

Jones left the casino to join a companion that he was staying with while in Monte Carlo. Her name was Lollita Baudou, the daughter of French Ambassador Phillip Baudou. Miss Baudou was a very attractive blond with large brown eyes and large creamy white bosom. She was rather tall at five-foot eight. When she heard of the dual she begged Jones to withdraw. She was in love with him and couldn't bear the thought of losing him. Jones was not in love with her, however, or any other woman for that matter. He was just using her to, eventually, extort money from her father. She was another plaything to occupy his daytime hours when he was not gambling. The desire to be loved by a woman was his only real weakness. He could easily have fallen in love with several of his young victims and it was very difficult for him to reject them. He knew if he didn't spurn them he would become a failure at his trade. He made love with Lollita for the last time that morning and then rested in her arms for several hours before his dual.

It was clear that evening with a little breeze from the sea. The two of them squared off while their seconds looked on. For the last six years Jones traveled with his gentleman's gentleman, John Wilson, who was not really concerned for Mr. Jones's safety because he knew of his employer's talents. In any confrontation Jones would always look for an advantage and since he had the choice he selected to face his opponent from the west. The sun was just about in the right position by now setting slowly behind the hills. He knew it would help to obscure the German's vision. The neutral judge stood up and made his final announcement.

"Are you ready." They both nodded. "If either of you wish to stop this insane dual you may still do so. No one would hold it against you." Neither budged.

"Very well then, at my first count you will both begin walking ten paces in opposite directions and turn and shoot at the count of ten. I will count out the paces out loud. If either of you turns to shoot before I announce the tenth step you will be shot dead on the spot by my men. Do you understand these rules?" No answer.

"Very well then, may God have mercy on your souls."

At the initial count the two men began walking apart taking one step at a time as the judge counted out the steps out loud. When the judge reached ten they both whirled and shot at the same time. They both fell to the ground. Jones was shot in the left shoulder but Miller was dead with a bullet hole neatly placed in his forehead symmetrically spaced between his eyes. Jones once again proved that he was still a deadly shot.   He   was helped up by his valet, John Wilson, who assisted him to the carriage. He was treated that evening by a doctor and the next night he was back at the gambling tables with a sling over his left arm. Lollita was at his side gambling with him. To his surprise he was actually congratulated by many at the tables for eliminating Miller who wasn't particularly admired in these circles.

At the Roulette table he began winning, as usual, but the manager had his suspicions that Jones was winning illegally and called in the Gendarmes. He was challenged by the police after being pulled to one side. He was told to leave Monte Carlo or spend some time in jail. They had several cases of crooked gamblers infiltrating the casinos before so their practice was simply to eliminate the person immediately. They didn't have to show just cause and could remove anyone from the table for any reason what-so-ever. Bismarck chose to leave for America after deciding that he had already accumulated a profitable sum of cash during this gambling trip. He told Lollita that he would be back in a month but he knew he wouldn't. She cried as he left her. This was always the hardest thing for him to do, to leave a beautiful girl crying. His emotions for her were truly genuine. He never did get to extort money from her father which was really his only real sorrow. He knew when it was time to fold.

He booked passage back to the States on the Mauretania, which happened to be anchored at the port city of Nice. He secured first class tickets for himself and his valet. While they were riding to Nice by a horse driven cab, Jones said to his valet,

"You know John, Karl Miller called me Bismarck. I think I wouldn't mind using that as a nicknamed. It has a certain sophisticated ring to it. What do you think?"

"I agree, sir. It certainly is a better nickname than what others have been calling you lately, and it's definitely better than what those other American hustlers are being called; such as Count Yogi, Fat Stanawitz, Slim Parkins, and Titanic Thompson."

And so, henceforth, William Jones will be known as Bismarck Jones.

After the Mauretania left its mooring and was well out to sea, Bismarck would take brief walks around the upper deck to observe the different passengers. He was especially interested in older women, preferably rich widows. They would be much easier to prey upon by such a professional Con artist like himself.

Bismarck Jones was slim of figure at six feet two inches and was rather good looking with wavy brown hair, a thin mustache that was perfectly trimmed, and had exceptionally penetrating blue eyes that sometimes worked against him. His pale face was clean shaven and always looked distinguished in his tailor made suits. He could easily pass for a professional business man. He was always dressed eloquently in the presence of strangers with either a grey or navy blue suit, white shirt and matching tie. Being a well traveled man he could easily hold a conversation with anyone on just about any subject. He was careful, however, not to reveal too much of himself or he might be detected as a phony. He could speak eight languages fair enough to get by but was profusely in German, French, Spanish and, of course, English.

His approach to older women was rather simple. He encouraged them to do most of the talking and they would eventually reveal their financial status. He knew that he was exceptionally attractive to older women, especially when he wore his disguise. Most of the women couldn't resist having a conversation with him and they would casually pass hints that they were well off financially hoping that they could entice him into having dinner with them and possibly a follow on love affair. He knew how to play the game, that's for sure.

Bismarck had already concluded that there were two types of women in the first class section, married women who wanted to have a short fling while on this cruise but would immediately go back to their husbands as soon as they docked, and women that are truly lonely either widowed or never have been married. He would never use the word spinster because it had the connotation that they were homely and could never meet a proper gentleman. He preferred the widows because they usually inherited large fortunes and were the easiest to prey upon. Bismarck's experience with widows taught him that most of them never learned how to handle their finances during their marriage, and when their husbands died they were left with this awful burden. Bismarck was always there to help these poor unfortunate women by investing their savings in very profitably ventures. Profitable for himself, that is.

Most of the time he would research his victims very carefully before he would approach them, but on a short cruise such as this there wasn't enough time, so he had to resort to his ingenuity. He would avoid, at all costs, young pretty women. All they wanted was a good time or get married. Young women were considered taboo in the confidence racket. Too many excellent hustlers had fallen for a pretty face and were destroyed because of it. Having an occasional affair with a young lady was permissible but for one night stands only. He was living with Lollita for a week and if it wasn't for the police he may have married her. That was a close call. On a cruise such as this a young pretty girl would have hounded him to death and would want more than just to spend one night in the sack. No, he had to stick with the older and more mature women if he is to score.

Bismarck was not born a hustler. It all started when he was twelve years old in the sixth grade in Shimer Junior High School in Queens, New York. His parents were considered middle class during the depression because his Dad worked for the city as an electrician in the subway system. They were not rich but they lived in an attached brick home complex in South Ozone Park and were very comfortable. His mom would give him twenty cents every day to buy his lunch at the school cafeteria. One day a large black boy, Leroy Jackson, approached him and threatened him with bodily harm if he didn't give him half of his lunch money.

"This is protection money, kid."

"Who are you protecting me from?" asked William.

"From me, dummy."

That's when he discovered the many different rackets that were going on at his school. Eventually, Leroy was turned in by one of the other students and was expelled from school. Leroy was over the state age limit of sixteen years for mandatory schooling so it was no problem expelling him.

Then there was a junior high school senior, Mario Donatelli, who ran a neat gambling racket. He would take bets for anything. If one wanted to bet on the New York Giants football team, for example, he would pay out seventy five cents for each dollar bet. He would also do the same on a bet for the opposing team, so if he had the same number of betters from both sides he would always be guaranteed a buck and a quarter on any two opposing bets. He would even take bets for half time scores.

During the baseball season Mario would pay two to one if a boy bet on a total of six hits or more from three players on different teams that they selected that day. He sometimes got hurt on that bet because everyone would select Babe Ruth or Lou Gehrig as one of the players. He would also give odds on the spread in the final score of a game and even gave combinational bets on horses.

He also took bets on the numbers racket that were published in the New York Daily News each day. For a quarter he would pay fifty dollars if anyone hit all the numbers. Fortunately, it was a very long shot and he never had to pay off. Almost all of the students played the numbers including the girls. He conned the students by making believe a different student would hit the numbers every month. The winning student was a set-up and was given five bucks to fake the win. Sometimes the same student would fake winning more than once.

Because Mario was so busy taking bets before classes or during the lunch break he had to hire four other students to help collect the bets and record them. He paid off the winners every morning on bets made the day before or on Monday mornings for Friday bets.

Before long William was using half his lunch money to place bets with Mario. After awhile he became so efficient at it he didn't have to use his lunch money anymore. Mario was getting wise to this kid who was always winning so he refused him bets and, instead, made William a runner to collect bets. William was paid quite well. As a runner he learned all about the trade of gambling. When Mario graduated to high school William took over the racket in the eighth grade. His mom and dad couldn't understand how he made so much money. He just told them that he was working after school. His racketeering continued all through high school and later on in the streets.

He was eventually picked up by the police and warned that if he was caught at it again it meant reform school, so he had to resort to other forms of gambling. He became an excellent pool shark and golfer. He started hustling people at the pool tables throughout the five New York Boroughs. He eventually had to leave the city because his reputation as a pool hustler was getting pretty well known.

He learned to shoot a gun when he worked at a Coney Island shooting gallery. He would bet the customers on the side that he could out-shoot them at moving targets and, of course, he always won. The extra side betting practically stop because he was always winning, so then he bet them he could beat them blindfolded and later on behind his back with a mirror. He still won, of course. He later went on the road to different states to gamble and challenge anyone with his twenty-two pistols and rifles. He was amazing. In whatever venture he undertook he always became proficient at it and used his talents for one purpose only, to hustle money.

On all of his spare time he would practice his pistol shooting, playing card tricks, golf, pool playing, baseball, basketball and football. All of his practicing was for one purpose only, hustling and gambling. In baseball he'd bet a professional player one hundred dollars even money that he could throw a ball from shallow center field through a tire hoop at home plate. He won easily. He did this feat many times in different towns to make extra money. William would do the same thing with a football except it was throwing it from second base. In basketball he would challenge anyone he could out-shoot them in consecutive foul shots. He did the same thing at the top of the key with his old fashion two handed set shot.

With all of his capabilities Jones never became interested in any one sport. It was only for the fun of it and, of course, the joy of winning the money by outsmarting his opponent. This was the greatest thrill for Bismarck, to hustle a target and then take him to the cleaners with a big bet. It became an obsession with him.

One evening in his motel room another gambler was having a drink with him when William said, "You see that fly on the wall. I'll bet you a hundred bucks even money that I can hit and kill it with a cube of ice thrown from this chair."

The man look up and saw the fly setting there and estimated the distance was fifteen feet away and concluded it would be impossible for him to do it. "Your on, Bill."

Bismarck reached into the ice bucket removed a cube and showed it to his guest. He then pulled his arm back and threw the cube at the fly which promptly fell to the floor dead. The guest walked over and picked up the fly and examined it. Sure enough it was dead. He paid Bismarck off but still couldn't believe he did it. Bismarck was nobody's fool. Whenever he made a bet he made sure he would win. He had previously place the dead fly on that wall that was barely hanging on by a thin thread. The slightest movement next to the fly would cause it to drop to the floor. He practiced it for several hours and was waiting for the right sucker to come along. It was easy money. He learned this trick from another famous hustler, Titanic Thompson.

When he was twenty-two years old he was invited by another hustler, Mr. Steven Nichols, to a country club in Long Island to play golf. The other hustler was an older man who was independently wealthy but liked to take on young punks like William and teach them a lesson. That's how he got his kicks.

Mr. Nichols was a man in his late forties. He was about five foot nine and was a little overweight. At one time he was considered a prospect as a professional golfer. He couldn't follow the circuit because he was too busy making a fortune with his automobile parts business. He owned a series of auto parts stores throughout the country and he grossed one hundred million dollars a year. He also inherited a rather large sum from his father, including a large estate in upstate New York. Playing golf was now mostly for the fun of it. He especially liked to challenge young and up coming pros and knock them down a peg. It became a personnel vendetta for him after he was once defeated and ridiculed by a young pro who became popular on the PGA tour. He then decided to take the game up more seriously so he would never be embarrassed like that again.

When he heard about this kid, who was hustling money at a pool hall, he decided to challenge him in a game of pool. Nichols was considered a pretty good pool player himself but when he tangled with William Jones he knew he met a professional hustler. The game cost him ten thousand dollars.

"Your pretty good at pool kid. Is there any other game you would like to play for money? How about golf?"

"Yeah. I play a little. But it's been awhile for me."

"How about a little contest of match play at my country club. It'll give me a chance to win some of my money back," challenged Mr. Nichols.

"Sure, why not," responded William who was trying to hold back his enthusiasm.

William drove up to the country club and was impressed. The first thing that came to his mind was old money. He walked into the club house and there was Nichols waiting talking to other rich members. William said to himself, "What a set up. I could make a living off of these old buzzards."

They played for ten dollars a hole with carry overs on ties and, of course, Jones intentionally lost one hundred dollars to this rich jerk who thought he was a better golfer.

William then asked, "Why don't we make it more interesting tomorrow and up the stakes to one hundred dollars a hole?"

Nichols naturally accepted the challenge after easily winning the first round. The next day William won sixteen out of eighteen holes and pocketed fourteen hundred bucks. Nichols was furious.

In the club house and at the bar, William was bragging out

loud to the other members of the club on how easily he beat Mr. Nichols.

"I could beat that old fool left handed, Ha."

Nichols was seated at a table with a female guest when he overheard William's challenge and quickly walked over to the bar and announced, "That's a bet. You're on, for ten thousand dollars left handed for eighteen holes low score."

"Now wait a minute. I was only kidding. I never played left handed in my life."

"What's the matter. You were just shooting off your mouth that you could beat me left-handed, didn't you? Now let's see you prove it."

All of the other members agreed, "Put your money where your mouth is, Bill, or shut your damn trap around here."

William was in a bind. He had to accept the challenge or be disgraced and never be allowed to play on this course again. "Alright, you're on, Mr. Nichols, and anyone else who wants to bet against me."

Ten of the other members jumped at this chance of easy money and covered his bet. On the side later Mr. Nichols told the other members that he had purposely lost the second round to make Jones feel sure of himself to sucker him into a larger wager. He never expected Bill to take him on swinging left-handed, however. William was purposely acting reluctant about accepting the wagers from the other members so as not to give himself away.

He yelled out, "Hey, wait a minute. If I lose I'm out a hundred grand."

After further persuasion he finally agreed, but then said, "No more bets. That's all I can afford. Christ, I could go broke after this match."

William had to play it cool or they would have gotten wise to him. Most people don't like being taken early in a game so he had to delay his time for winning. On the first hole Nichols had a par. William could have easily birdie the hole but he had to take it easy. He purposely missed a three foot putt tying the hole. He did this for the next three holes and in each case he tied his opponent. He then made a birdie on the next three holes and after seven holes he was three strokes up. He purposely lost the eighth and ninth hole to make Nichols feel good. Nichols was now becoming aware that William was falling apart so he up's his bet to twenty thousand dollars. William reluctantly agreed. He then proceeded to birdie the next nine holes and walked away from that tournament winning a total of 120,000 dollars playing left-handed. William left town as soon as possible.

The Mauretania Affair

The Mauretania is the sister ship of the Lusitania which was sunk by the Germans in 1915. Both were launched in 1906 and the Mauretania remained a transport until 1935. On board the Mauritania, Bismarck continued his walks over the promenade deck and down to the lower decks, searching for the right target. He then saw her at the rear of the Promenade deck. He estimated she was a woman in her early fifties, probably a widow. She was sitting comfortably on a lounge chair with a blanket over her legs to protect her from the cool sea breezes. She had on reading glasses and was deeply absorbed in a book. She was not too slim of figure but was still rather attractive for her age. Bismarck noticed that she was holding her cabin key in her left hand as she read her book. He quickly put on his specially made glasses and was able to read her cabin number. He then went to the pursers office to ascertain her name. He later began a casual conversation with the porter who was assigned to take care of her cabin. The porter was a little man probably of Italian extraction. Bismarck took out a ten spot and asked him, "Do you happen to know if Mrs. Agnus Phillips is traveling alone?"

In somewhat broken English he answered, "Yes she is, sir. Her husband had passed away in America six months ago and she went to Europa to get away from it all. She is just now returning home." The porter was very eager to gain that ten spot and anxiously revealed all that he knew about Mrs. Phillips.

Bismarck just smiled and gave the porter the ten dollar bill. Money works wonders when one is trying to acquire information. He headed back to his own cabin to make adjustments on his appearance. His first class cabin was very large with large windows overlooking the ocean. There were two compartments side by side, the smaller one was for his valet. Bismarck had his own personal bar with all sorts of spirits and wines. There was enough beverages in the bar to run his own gambling table. Gambling was not on his mind at the moment.

He sometimes became bored using only one form of confidence game for making money. He needed a variety of Con games to satisfy his whims. Today it's extortion.

He immediately sat at his night table and opened up his special make-up kit. He began the tedious procedure of changing his looks. He knew that a fifty year old woman wouldn't particularly want to become involved with a twenty-eight year old man, so he needed the right disguise. He carefully enhanced the crows marks around his eyes, put on his slightly greying beard and covered his pencil mustache with a larger grey one. He had to cut his own hair shorter so that the grey wig would not be too obvious. He topped off his disguise with his specially made glasses.

These were not just ordinary glasses. The left lens was made of plain glass but the right lens was a trifocal. The upper portion of the trifocal was plain glass, the center slit was for long distance with ten to one magnification. This is how he was able to read the cabin number on Mrs. Phillips key from a distance. The lower lens was for close distances so that he could examine the back of an opponent's marked cards to tell what card they had.

He developed a special technique of card marking after many years of trial an error. What he would do was to tape a razor sharp object to his right forefinger and would scratch his personal code on the back of the cards. An ace, for example, would have one scratch, a king would have an X scratched on it, and queen would have two scratches on it, etc. These scratches would not be visible to the naked eye, but with his special high powered lens he could easily distinguish them. His only problem was when he was playing against a professional, the "Pro" instinctively would cup the cards in his hands so that the back of the cards were not visible. Every Pro knew of the many different illegal tricks and assumed everyone else he played against was as crooked as he was. This is how Bismarck first detected that Karl Miller was a Pro when he watched him play the previous evening before their dual at Monte Carlo.

Earlier in his career several players refused to play with Bismarck because of the tape he had on his finger so he went to a plastic surgeon and had a special metal permanently inserted in his right forefinger. The metal contained a grove which Bismarck used to insert his razor sharp tool or replace it whenever it became dull. He always inserted the blade just a few minutes before game time.

When Karl Miller was watching Bismarck's last game he couldn't detect how Jones was marking the cards but he knew it was taken place. Bismarck's approach was rather simple, whenever he received cards he would mark them as they were cupped in his own hand. In order for this technique to work he would have to sit through several hands making small bets. When enough cards were marked he would then make very large bets as long as he knew he had a winning hand.

In his last game, previous to the dual, he was losing a thousand dollars in draw poker and one of the aristocratic players opened the next hand with a bet of five hundred dollars. Bismarck could easily read the back of the man's cards as he held them loosely. He was definitely not a Pro. The man had two aces, a king, and two other unmarked cards. Bismarck had three duces so he raised and doubled the bet. The man called and drew only two cards saving the king as a kicker, hoping to bluff the rest of the players into thinking he had three of a kind. He drew another king giving him two pair. There was one other player who stayed in the game who drew three cards. Bismarck asked for one card indicating that he possibly had two of a kind. The first man began betting and raising heavily and Bismarck kept up with him. Finally the third man dropped out.

Bismarck could see that the man, who was still in the game, had drawn another king so he was sure that his three duces would still beat his two pair. There was already over ten thousand dollars on the table and Bismarck's last raise was for five thousand dollars. This was quite a sum in those days considering it would be equivalent to one hundred thousand American in 1990. The man was very uncomfortable. The stress was getting to him. His forehead and neck began sweating and he wiped himself constantly with a handkerchief. He was sure that his aces over kings would beat any two of a kind that Bismarck might have unless he filled in with a full house. The odds of that happening were slim but one can never be sure, he thought. He finally called. Bismarck turned over his three duces and paused for a moment to allow his opponent time to acknowledge that he had won. Bismarck saw the disappointment on his opponents face and new for sure he had won. He then pulled in all of the chips while trying to show no emotion over his big win.

After such a win the rest of the players would normally ask for a new deck of cards so Bismarck would have to go through the tedious ritual of marking the new set of cards all over again. He was patient, however, and knew that time was on his side so he would go back to making small bets again while he was marking the new cards.

In his cabin Bismarck stood up and examined himself in a full length mirror. He turned left and then right. He was quite pleased with himself.

"What'a you think, John? Can I pass myself off as a fifty year old business man?"

"Sir. You look perfect."

He then headed out to the rear of the Promenade deck to meet his quarry. He came to the chair where she was staying and was somewhat disturb. She was not there.

He said to himself, "Don't panic, Bill. Take your time. She may have gone back to her cabin." He began walking towards her cabin when he stumbled into her as she was coming out on deck.

"I beg your pardon, Madam. It was very clumsy of me."

"Oh, that's alright. It was really my fault. I'm not used to riding on ships with so many people around."

He took the opportunity and said, "May I introduce myself. My name is William Jones from New York. I'm coming back to the States after having a very successful business investment abroad. You see, I'm an investment broker and I do travel a lot."

"Oh. That's very interesting, Mr. Jones. I'm Mrs. Agnus Phillips and I recently lost my husband," making sure he caught her misfortune. She looked him over carefully and was quite impressed with his appearance and mannerism.

"Mrs. Phillips. I have to confess that I've been admiring you ever since we left France. You strike me as a very happy person who has had a wonderful married life. I'm sorry for your loss. He must have been a wonderful man to have been married to such an attractive woman as yourself."

"Well, thank you Mr. Jones. That was kind of you to say that, but I have finally accepted my husband's death and this trip helped me a lot."

"If I may be so bold, Mrs. Phillips, may we have lunch together? You see, I am also single. My wife divorced me ten years ago and it would be nice to talk to someone closer to my own age. The trip could be awfully boring, alone."

"Well, I suppose it would make the trip a little more interesting. Yes, thank you Mr. Jones. I will be delighted to join you for lunch."

"The first thing I insist on, Mrs. Phillips, is that you call me William as most of my friends do."

"I will if you will call me Agnus." They both agreed and smiled at each other. They began casually walking the deck together with her hand under his arm.

Agnus couldn't believe her luck. All the while she was in Europe she hadn't made any acquaintances with an older male. She wasn't particularly looking for a husband, but she would have enjoyed a male companion to ease her depression over losing her husband. Agnus was about five foot two and was slightly overweight but very acceptable in Bismarck's eyes. She presented an alluring smile with her white teeth which complemented her attractive small rounded face. She had blond hair that blended well with her slightly greying hair. There was no doubt about it she was rather good looking for her age and Bismarck wouldn't mind bedding her. He's had much worse before.

Bismarck was careful. He took his time. Patience was his greatest asset. They had their lunch and later that evening they had dinner together. Bismarck ordered champaign. The orchestra began playing a slow tune and Bismarck asked her for a dance which she quickly accepted. At first Bismarck kept his distance but slowly he moved in closer. She didn't stop him and in no time they were very close. Bismarck could see that she was really enjoying herself and grinned. He knew she was an easy target. A lonely woman with plenty of money. Why shouldn't she share it with a man who was willing to make her happy, he reasoned.

That night Bismarck almost goofed by trying too hard to bed her on the first night. She was not that sort of a woman, he was told. So he waited. There's plenty of time he concluded. The next night he tried again and this time she let him, at least, come into her cabin for a nightcap. As Bismarck entered he noticed that her cabin was rather small in comparison to his but adequate for two adults. The walls were made of expensive mahogany panelling and there was a large port hole next to the bed facing the ocean. He noticed a king size bed was in the center of the cabin with a table and two chairs along side near the port hole. Agnus poured two glass of wine and they sat at the table. The conversation was one sided and mostly about her former husband. Bismarck let her do all the talking. It was the way he operated.

After they had a couple of drinks Bismarck pretended to be impatient and stood up to leave. She couldn't understand why he wanted to leave so soon. As they approach the door Bismarck put his arms around her and began kissing her. She at first rebelled but then gave in to his kisses. Bismarck apologized for being so forward.

"I'm sorry Agnus, I couldn't help myself. You must think I'm a cad. Please forgive me."

"There is nothing to forgive, William. You are a red blooded American man, and men do sometimes get a little rambunctious. Now, it might be a good idea that you do leave before we are both sorry." As Bismarck stepped to the door he slowly turned and kissed her again. She didn't refuse him.

The next night he tried once more to bed her and this time he was successful. As they were removing their clothes, Bismarck lowered the lights and said that he preferred it that way. His main reason was so that she wouldn't detect his young body even though he had grayed the hair on his chest. When she was naked he was delighted that she had a rather attractive body and her breasts were not sagging too badly. He had made love to many older women and sometimes they were down right fat and grotesque. But she wasn't too bad. Just slightly overweight. He wanted to mount her right away but she stopped him because she first wanted to provide him with special sex. She said older men sometimes need a little stimulation to attain a good erection. Bismarck rather enjoyed this unexpected behavior. When she saw that he was ready she then allowed him to enter her and in no time at all they both reach ecstacy together. It's been awhile for her. She was very pleased with his performance but she wouldn't allow him to spend the night, at least not just yet. Bismarck was thankful for that and left.

The next night he made excuses of not to going to bed with her by saying he's not the man he used to be. She could readily understand that condition because her late husband was much older than her and sometimes it was months before they had sex together.

After the fourth day at sea Bismarck began receiving wireless cablegrams from New York. He always made sure that the grams were given to him at the dinner table so Agnus would witness them. He paid a stewart ten bucks each time he delivered a false cablegram.

"Is it good or bad news, William?"

"Very good news. My investments on Wall Street are doing quite well. Are you in the stock market, my dear Agnus?"

"No I'm not. I don't know much about that sort of thing. You see my late husband, George, took care of all our investments. I wouldn't know where to begin."

"Well, I just purchased one hundred thousand dollars of Colonial Oil (no such company) and you might want to consider it. You should be able to double your money in a month."

"Do you really think I could, William? Should I equal your investment?"

"No, my dear. I think you should try it out first with a small investment. You know, the stock market is not for everyone. There is always a risk. Here's what you should do. Invest only say a thousand dollars and see how it goes. Then maybe after you become a little better at it you might think about investing more, but not just yet, my love." What a set up. Bismarck was at his best.

"Alright, I'll do it. Will you handle it for me, William? I simply don't know where to begin."

"Certainly, precious. If you will write out a check for one thousand dollars payable to me I will purchase the stock and handle all the details for you."

Agnus did write out the check and Bismarck, of course, just pocketed it temporarily. Early the next morning Bismarck knocked on her cabin door. She was still in bed and asked who was it?

"It's me, William. I have great news." After she opened the door he said, "Honey, you have already doubled your money. I sold the stock immediately and look, two thousand dollars in cash and it's all yours."

"Oh my goodness. It's so exciting. Won't you take some? After all you made it possible."

"Agnus, please don't insult me like that. Besides, I sold my shares and made two hundred thousand dollars profit myself. Isn't that great?"

He then put his arms around her and kissed her passionately. In no time at all they were back in bed making love. She couldn't believe how lucky she is meeting this wonderful man. He is an outstanding lover and could also handle her investments for her. She hoped it wasn't just a dream, and if it was she didn't want to wake up.

They reached the New York Harbor the next evening and Bismarck said that he will have to find a hotel for himself so there was no way, at the moment, that she could get in touch with him. He said he will call her at her home in Connecticut in a day or so, which he did. In order for his Con game to work he had to let her raise the price of her investments slowly so that she would feel secure enough and be willing to invest a large sum for him to make the kill. This meant that he would have to have a large bank account of his own to cover her erroneous winnings. It took about three months to work up her investment to a million dollars. Meantime, he was out three hundred thousand dollars by letting her think she was making a lot of money in the stock market. The last and final investment came on her birthday, and he told her it was a good omen and that she could make a fortune on this glorious day.

As she had done many times before she deposited the one million dollars into Bismarck's bank account for him to invest. He waited two weeks to make sure the transaction was completed and was accepted by his own bank. Bismarck then made his move and removed all but ten thousand dollars from his account. He later went to a friend who was the manager of the Laslo Manhattan bank and transferred the remainder of the million dollars to a Geneva bank in Switzerland. He paid his buddy twenty thousand dollars to handle the transaction. Bismarck then left town and Agnus never saw him again. Actually, she saw him many times there-after but she wouldn't recognize him without his beard and grey hair. Bismarck also wore dark glasses when he was around her because he knew that she might recognize his unusual blue eyes which might give him away. He also toyed with the idea of possibly hustling her again. She could well afford another hit he speculated but he didn't.

The Invitations

Several years later on a cool fall afternoon Mrs. Phillips was pruning her roses when the mailman arrived with her mail.

"Good afternoon Mrs. Phillips, and how are you feeling this wonderful day."

"Fine, Mr. Brown. More bills I see."

"There's one here that doesn't look like a bill, Mrs. Phillips."

Mrs. Phillips examined the envelope. The return address and sender were not familiar to her. It was from a Mr. Steven Nichols. She immediately opened it and read its contents:

Dear Mrs. Phillips:

"You don't know me but I believe we have a mutual friend who is known by several names such as William Jones, Bismarck Jones, or Bill Jones. Mr. Jones is probably the greatest hustler and Con artist the world has ever known and for many years he has preyed upon many innocent people, especially mature widows like yourself. After he had hustled me and my friends in a golf match six years ago, I hired a man to spy on him. He's an incredible swindler and I think it is now time for us to get even with this man. My spy has been keeping tabs on him and has recorded all of his crooked activities and he gave me a list of all the people that had been swindled. I still have that list and that is how I acquired your name.

"What I am proposing to do is to have a meeting with all of the people that have been fleeced by this Mr. Jones to discuss our association with him and how he jilted each and everyone of us out of our substantial savings. We also want to discuss ways and means to obtain a suitable revenge. I have tried many times to have him indicted as a criminal but the authorities continuously have told me there wasn't enough evidence to convict him. So he remains a free man preying on other unfortunate people. I understand he has used his confidence money wisely on several legitimate investments and has now become a multi-millionaire.

"I am now inviting you as my guest to come to this meeting with all expenses paid by me. My estate is in Hyde Park, New York, overlooking the Hudson River near the birth place of President Roosevelt. Mrs. Phillips, I cannot tell you how important it is for you to attend because I'm at the brink of breaking this individual and I intend to prevent this despicable confidence man from ever preying upon another poor soul again. I'll be looking forward to meeting you January 13, 1934, to hear your story on how he extracted money from you. I have a plan in mind to trap him at his own game and to extract millions from him, but I will need your assistance and the help of all the other individuals that he has bamboozled."

Sincerely,
Steven Nichols.

January 13 was a Friday and by coincidence only thirteen people showed up at Hyde Park. Steven Nichols had sent letters to fifteen different people who were hustled out of money one way or another by Bismarck. All but two have responded and agreed to attend his meeting. Most of them arrived that Thursday because they had to travel great distances including Europe, and they didn't want to become involved in a meeting the same day they arrived. Being early actually turned out to be a better choice for them because they were able to introduce themselves informally and become more acquainted with each other.

As each guest arrived at the main gate they were driven to the mansion by horse and buggy. The property was enormous and the house was located one/half mile from the street. There were huge trees of different varieties on the land as far as one can see. Even though the trees were bare the property looked more like a forest. There was a narrow stone horse path leading to the main building. The front of the brick building had huge white columns extending thirty feet high to an over-hanging contoured roof. The vestibule floor was laid with imported Italian white tile that were spotlessly cleaned. The back of the estate overlooked the Hudson River that was about one hundred feet below. It was quit a view. To the right of the mansion was a large brick building that could resemble a guest house but was actually the stables.

The first to arrive was a gentleman and a lady from Italy. His name was Count Rocco Marabito. He was accompanied by his twenty-five year old lovely daughter, Lisa, who was, in fact, taking care of him. Rocco was in his late seventies by now and was not in the best of health. She also acted as his interpreter.

The guests that arrived that first day were; Mr. James Barnum also known a Slick Barny from Brooklyn, Mrs. Mary Elsworth from England, Mr. Edward Young from Australia, Mr. John Watts from San Francisco, Mr. and Mrs. Harold Schwartz from Florida, Pietro Columbo who was considered by many as the Mafia boss of Manhattan, Mrs. Angela Wagner from Ohio, and Max Keller from Germany. The rest of the guests were expected to arrived the next day.

When Count Rocco and his daughter arrived the first thing the butler did was escort them to separate but adjoining rooms. The count was pleased with the accommodations because the large rooms were very European in style except with oak furniture instead of mahogany. An hour later Countessa Lisa came down to the main living room which was brightened by the Sun through a skylight located at the roof top of the two story building. Not only did the Sun provide light it helped heat the main living room by convection as in a hot house. She was offered a glass of champaign by the butler. She began strolling through the house holding her glass and casually observing the different European paintings on the walls. Suddenly she heard yelling at the front door. It was Slick Barny arguing with the butler about his brief case. The butler was merely trying to store it for him but Slick wouldn't allow that.

"I told you, Ass-hole, this briefcase stays with me wherever I go. Now, bug-off!"

"Very good, Sir."

Then Slick looked up and saw Lisa. He was stunned. He couldn't believe his eyes. All of a sudden his mannerism changed and he walked up to her and said, "Hi baby. Are you the hostess of this outfit?"

"Oh no. I'm a guest here myself."

"Well, I'm please to make your acquaintance. I'm also a guest. My name is James Barnum, but you can call me Slick."

Slick was drooling at the mouth, looking over her figure as though he was examining a new applicant for a chorus line. She was exceptionally pretty and did have a fine figure. Her slightly exposed large breasts complemented her rather tall body of five foot eight inches. She had pure white skin with a rather small round face and had long reddish brown hair. She had large light blue eyes which was common among the royalties of Italy as they intermarried with other Europeans. She knew that she was exceptionally attractive and used her alluring smile and figure to attract many a noble in Europe. Although she had many suitors she never married because she was still looking for mister perfect and for other unfortunate reasons which she kept to herself. While she stood there holding her champaign glass in a sophisticated manner, she looked down at this thin uncouth person who tried to passed himself off as a desirable suitor. She obviously detested him right from the start.

"I am Countessa Lisa Marabito, from Milan," she announced and then turned abruptly lifting her head high and went back into the living room.

Slick felt a little snubbed and moved his head back and forth mimicking her as she walked back to the large room. He figured eventually she will come around and be his lover. Most of the girls from the lower section of Brooklyn were crazy about him, not because of his charm or looks but because he was always flashing a wad of money in the neighborhood. Slick was also an accomplished hustler himself but he lost a bundle when he locked horns with Bismarck. The butler finally asked him to follow him to his room.

Rocco Marabito was a Count in name only, losing his title when the fascists took over Italy. After being swindled by Bismarck and making a few of his own poor investments he had lost almost all of his assets. He was hoping to redeem himself financially through this meeting with Mr. Nichols so that he may someday provide a secure and proper estate for his daughter before he himself passed on. He had lost his wife, Helda, five years ago and now his own health was failing.

Bismarck was not a completely heartless person. Whenever he swindled money from a mark he would always make sure that that person had enough left over to continue to live a normal life. He never intended to reduce any person into bankruptcy. As a matter of fact, in one of his capers, he waited until one of his marks recouped himself and later was able to hustled him again, but he still left the man with enough assets to recoup himself again. Bismarck believed he was a considerate man and would never hurt anyone.

The next guest that arrived was Mrs. Mary Elsworth who was a widow in her fifties and was one of Bismarck's last clients. She was a large woman, tall, with an enormous bust line. Bismarck was unsuccessful in extorting money out of her but she was looking for him for other reasons. She was extremely wealthy from the garment business her husband had left her in England and her business was still doing exceptionally well. The only reason she agreed to attend this meeting was to find him. Bismarck was the only man that provided her with fruitful love and she wanted him back. She was secretly in love with him and would pay a substantial amount of money just to know of his whereabouts.

Bismarck had so many disguises that none of the people that arrived knew exactly what he actually looked like. They only remembered his appearance the last time they saw him. There were only three people who knew his true identity, his valet, Steven Nichols, and a certain young lady he met in Ireland who should arrive later. The older ladies still pictured him as a fifty to sixty year old man.

When Pietro Columbo, the Mafia chief, arrived he acted as though he owned the place. He was alleged to have been robbed of a five-million dollars worth of Cocaine by Bismarck. He now plans to have it returned and to exterminate Jones as a warning to others. His story will be very interesting because Bismarck had already eluded many attempts on his life from Columbo's hit-men.

One by one the majority of the guests were arriving. The final man to arrive that day was Max Keller. Max was actually Hans Miller, the brother of Karl Miller who Bismarck had killed in a dual. Hans was the only person in the group that was not hustled by Bismarck. All he wanted was revenge for the death of his brother. He was even larger than Karl, over six-foot five in height and weighed in at 300 pounds. He wasn't invited to this meeting directly, but had learned about it through the real Max Keller who was invited but couldn't make it himself. Hans Miller then introduced himself as Max Keller. Nothing else went on that day except the guest had introduced themselves and became more acquainted with each other.

The next day a pretty young lady arrived. Her name was Catherine Sullivan from Ireland. This was a bit unusual because most of the other guests were much older. She was actually representing her aunt who was swindled by Bismarck. Cathy was the only other person who ever saw William's true face though she didn't know at the time that he was the great Bismarck the notorious swindler. She was in love with him. It was one of the few times that Bismarck broke his vow not to become involved with a young lady, especially when he was on a caper against her aunt. But this turned out to be an unusual situation which he couldn't resist. While he was courting Cathy he had swindled her aunt out of 200,000 pounds. Bismarck felt remorse about leaving her because he also had feelings towards her. He even thought about marring her, but business comes first. Another close call.

Cathy was an exceptional pretty girl. She had long blond hair that laid softly on her shoulders. She had large brown eyes that seemed to sparkle when she talked. She was a bit short at five-foot two but had an outstanding figure with an adequate bust line. Cathy wore a long tight dress that constrained her movement which required her to take short steps as she walked among the other guests. The dress flared out at the ankles and would twirl forward as she walked which made her appear even more seductive to the men. Bismarck never forgot her and neither did she ever forget him. Her goal was not so much to have her aunt's money returned but she just wanted to find him. She was in love with him and would do anything to get him back. She had hoped that Mr. Nichols might help her locate him. When she had first walked in Slick made the same derogatory remarks he made to Lisa and she gave him the same cold treatment.

He uttered, "Bitch," as she walked away from him. Cathy simply ignored him. He was very crude and not even worth a response.

During that day the various guests were still becoming more acquainted with each other but they were all curious as to how Mr. Nichols planed to retaliate and regain their losses from this man called Bismarck Jones. That evening the guests were still waiting to meet Mr. Nichols and were getting impatient. Who is he and why is he so secretive? The butler then announced that dinner was now being served. As they all entered the dining room they saw names neatly placed on a long table as each person was pre-assigned to a chair. The dining room was very long and could easily accommodate 100 guests. The tables were designed with fold down leafs and when they were unfolded and butted together they could be extended into any length desired. When everyone was seated conversations between the guests became rather noisy. Finally the butler announce Mr. Nichols's arrival. All of a sudden there was a hush. The room became quiet as they all observed the entrance. He then stepped into the room and took a position at the head of the table. He stood there for a moment overlooking his various guests and not saying a word. It was an eerie sensation for all.

He then began to speak, "Good evening, ladies and gentleman. I hope that everything is to your satisfaction." He smiled at the crowd and slowly raised his glass to present a toast.

"To Mr. Bismarck Jones, the greatest confidence man in the world."

None of the guests would acknowledge his toast because they didn't understand his reasons and some despised Bismarck.

Why would they toast him when they were all victims of his conniving and crooked activities.

"I see you don't understand why I'm toasting him. Well, as you know from my invitations I was tracking him for the last six years and I too detest him, but as I have followed his activities I later began to have a different view of this man. He was so cunning and shrewd that I couldn't help but respect the way he manipulated both men and woman and duped you all out of your savings. I actually began to marvel this man. Don't misunderstand me, this doesn't alter my purpose here of beating him at his own game. I still want my revenge. Please enjoy your dinner and later we will discuss my plan. I want to thank each and every one of you for being here. Some of you came from great distances and, believe me, I appreciate your effort. Thank you again for coming." With that last statement Nichols sat down as dinner was being served.

The Meeting of the Victims

After dinner all of the guests retired to the main living room and began conversing over different subjects while Mr. Nichols stood by a fire place that was burning rather low. He was somewhat ammused watching his guests malling around each trying to act important.

He finally addressed his guests, "Ladies and Gentlemen. May I have your attention." After a short pause the room began to settled down. He began speaking again, "Before we begin discussing anything, I would like to introduce to you at this time the private investigator I hired to track Mr. Jones for the past six years. Ladies and gentlemen, meet Mr. John Wilson."

Mr. Wilson walked into the room and all of the guests immediately recognized him as Bismarck's personnel valet. They were astonished.

Mr. Nichols continued his comments, "I see you all recognize Mr. Wilson. I knew you would. You see, when I undertake a task I do it right. When someone crosses me there is no limit in expenses that I will use to avenge myself. I have ruined many a fraud or overly ambitious person who had tried to take advantage of me. It's just a little harder with this one because he is such a successful scoundrel and is very cautious. However, now is the time to strike back. Mr. Wilson, will you please give my guests a brief summary on how you were able to become Mr. Jones's right hand man."

"Thank you, Mr. Nichols. A scoundrel he certainly is, sir. In all of my years as a detective I have never met such an accomplished confidence man. Not only is he a crook but he has exceptional talent in so many different endeavors. In whatever subject you may think of, if there is a dollar to be made, Bismarck Jones knows how to make it. He is a polished conniver, a manipulator, a hustler, and the most successful confidence man that history has ever known, and believe me, I've seen them all. By the way, Bismarck is his nickname.

"When Mr. Nichols first hired me I didn't know how I was going to stay close enough to Bismarck without being detected. It was a stroke of luck that I did. We were on a Mississippi river gambling boat, the Missouri, heading down the river to New Orleans when I was observing Bismarck gambling in the lounge. He was winning handily at seven card stud when one of the losing players became suspicious. The man left the table disgruntled and about ten minutes later he came back with a gun.

"The man yelled out, `You're a crook, Jones. You took my life savings.' He then raise his gun and was about to shoot Bismarck. I immediately grabbed for the gun but it went off and the bullet struck Bismarck in the leg. Bismarck then wrestled the gun away from the man and quickly turned it toward him and shot the man dead through the heart. It all happened so fast I couldn't believe it. Bismarck was immediately attended to by the boat's physician. Later, when he saw me in the lounge, he asked me to join him for a drink at the bar, which I did.

"He asked me my name and I told him. I also said to him that he didn't have to kill that man even though he had every right to. He simply said to me, `Sir, one should never give a man a second chance. This man is now dead, so I don't have to be looking over my shoulder to see if he will try it again. It's that plain and simple. Now I want to thank you for what you did for me, Mr. Wilson. I'm usually more prepared for such incidences, but sometimes I have to rely on lady luck and this time you were my luck. You saved my life and I owe you. Can I pay you or do something for you.'

"I said to him that I'm out of work and could use a job. He then asked me if I don't mind traveling with him as his companion and be sort of a valet. He said he would take care of all of my expenses and pay me well. I could take two days off a week for my own interests because he was sure that I would like some time off to entertain a lady friend or whatever. I accepted. There was no better way for me to track him and observe his crooked dealings than by being his companion. How could I refuse? And, now I'm employed and being paid cash money by two different parties for the same job. Hah..." Forgetting himself momentarily, he glanced over at Mr. Nichols who wasn't laughing.

"Anyway, on one of those two days off I would always contact Mr. Nichols, whenever I could, and report all of Bismarck's latest ventures either by phone or by mail."

At this moment Nichols broke in and said, "Thank you Mr. Wilson. I'll take it from here. Yes, he did report to me promptly almost every Saturday except when they were on the high seas. He would then send me a cablegram. This is how I was able to get all of your names and learn how this rogue operates who was able to Con you out of your savings. Mr. Jones still doesn't know that John is working for me and I want him to continue his assignment until we break this bastard. Ah, excuse my language, ladies.

"Now, I want each and everyone of you to present your story to the rest of us on how Bismarck swindled you. It should be rather interesting and your story should help us in setting up our counter attack. Mrs. Phillips, will you be the first to enlighten us on all of your escapades with this scoundrel."

Mrs. Phillips stood up and began discussing her unfortunate experience with Bismarck on the Mauretania. Several times during her presentation she began to weep and finally finished by saying that she is still madly in love with him but wants him broken so that maybe he will come back to her. She had blushed when she mentioned that he was an excellent lover. This was typical of all of Bismarck's women conquests. They discovered later that he was a crook but they still want him back financially poor so that they will be able to have control of his life and continue to be their lover.

"Mrs. Phillips, can you describe Mr. Jones for us?" asked Mr. Nichols.

She did and finished by saying that no matter what disguise he uses she will always be able to recognize him because of his unusual blue eyes. "I have never seen another man with such fascinating blue eyes before. They are so beautiful," and swooned.

Bismarck did make that one mistake. He usually wears contact lenses with different colors for each of his ventures but that time he was at sea on the Mauretania and wasn't fully prepared because he lost some of his luggage in his haste to leave Monti Carlo.

Nichols then said, "You see, ladies and gentleman. This is how Bismarck operates. Only a few of us know what he actually looks like. That's why it is so difficult to prosecute him. Even John cannot be used as a witness because he had never actually witnessed Bismarck in the act of extorting anyone. He works alone. And besides, John is afraid of what this man would do to him. Bismarck can be very ruthless so he refuses to testify for fear of his own life."

John immediately responded, "Yes sir. I've seen this man in action and believe me if he had found out that I was a spy I wouldn't be here today." He was very convincing.

The Swindle of Count Rocco

The next person to speak is Count Rocco Marabito from Italy with his daughter Lisa, translating for him. Rocco is a rather large man but shorter than his daughter. Lisa inherited her height from her mother who was an Austrian aristocrat and a distant cousin to the suave and competent statesman Prince von Metternich of the eighteenth century. Rocco was completely bald and wore a grey goatee. Because of his weight he was always puffing and perspiring. Every movement seemed to be a major chore for him.

Rocco spoke in Italian from his chair but Lisa stood next to him translating his every word. She presented a very attractive figure standing there as though she was posing, tall, alluring and very business like. Both men and women couldn't help but admire her demeanor. The following story was translated by Lisa to the group:

It all began when Count Rocco was sailing into Genoa on his fifty foot yacht. As the yacht pulled up close to the pier there was a middle aged man standing on the dock with a brown briefcase. When they were tied up, a deck hand asked the man what he wanted.

"I would like to speak with Count Rocco. I have a very important message for him." The man handed the sailor a card who then took it through a cabin door on the lower deck. After a few moments the sailor came out and waved the man to come on board. The man simply scaled the railing on to the boat showing off his athletic ability. This was not a smart thing for Bismarck to do since he is now disguised as a much older man. The sailor was impressed but went back to work.

Bismarck entered the cabin door and met with the Count who was sitting on a bar stool with a robe on that partially covering a red bathing suit. He was smoking an Italian stoggy cigar. The bar was exceptionally large and could entertain as many as twenty people. Rocco casually looked over this bearded man of fifty or so who had on glasses and was dressed in an expensive tailor made grey suit. He could see that the fabric was made from the finest Italian woolen cloth.

"What can I do for you, signore?" said the count speaking in Italian.

The man answered in a rather crude but understandable Italian. "Your Excellency, my name is Pat Morgan from Ireland. I work for the Milano Investment Brokerage firm which handles all of your accounts. As a result of Mussolini and Hitler's new found powers, the world of investments is expected to change drastically. Consequently, my company has delegated me to discuss with you all of your European investments and to offer you a better and safer proposition to protect your interests. Is it safe to talk here, Your Excellency?"

"Yes, of course."

Bismarck then opened his briefcase and spread out a number of United State investment bonds on the bar. "You see, Your Excellency, our firm is gravely concerned over the current events now taken place in Europe. Because of the way Hitler and Mussolini are expanding we are afraid there is going to be another major war and it is possible that your investments will be lost, should the Allies win. There is no question in our minds that America will enter the war if Hitler gets out of hand. Since we have been taking care of your investments for the past twenty years we are concerned for you and your family. This is why I was sent here, to present to you a new portfolio of investments in the United States of America so that most of your property and money will be safe.

"What we are proposing is to transfer half of your European investments into safe negotiable bonds in the United States. In this way at least some of your investments will be safe should there be a war. You must admit that Hitler and Mussolini are on a rampage and it's only a matter of time when they will draw your country into a war. After studying the world powers of today we have come to the conclusion that if there is another world war Italy and Germany will lose."

"I disagree with you, signore. Italy and Germany are the two most powerful nations in the world. Together, we will conquer all of our enemies. Tell me, signore, what happens to my money if we win this so called new world war?"

"That's easy. If America and the Allies are conquered your investments will still be safe. You can claim them from America as the right of a leading Fascist. You see, Your Excellency, we know you are a member of the Fascist party."

"My God, nothing is secret anymore."

"By having half your investments in Europe and half in the United States you will always be assured of being at least half protected no matter who wins. Don't you agree, Your Excellency?"

"Yes. I suppose it does make sense. What do you wish me to do?"

"First of all, I want you to call my company to reassure yourself that I am a legitimate executor. Then my chauffeur will drive us to Milano and there you will remove from your safe deposit box in the Bank of Milano half of your present bonds that we have been talking about. We will then drive to my hotel where I will convert your European bonds into secured American bonds. It should take no more than four hours to accomplish this transaction. When we are through I will personally hand carry your converted bonds to be certified by the president of the Bank of Milano himself. There will be, of course, a fee for this transaction and you will be billed by my company later in the month. Are there any questions, Your Excellency?"

"No. I understand perfectly. I've had similar transactions like this before."

The count opened up a draw and produced an identification card from the Milano Investment Brokerage and began dialing the numbers on his ship to shore telephone. After a short conversation with the brokerage house Bismarck could tell that he was receiving satisfactory answers as the count was nodding his head as though he were talking to a person directly in front of him.

Bismarck was a master when preparing for a sting operation. He never left any loose ends and this caper was very carefully planned. He first had to investigate the Milano Brokerage house to determine who would be his next mark. He then had to assume the identity of a key man in the company. It took several weeks and many visits to the brokerage firm to select the right person and formulate the plan of attack. On his final visit to the firm he saw that an Irish executor, Pat Morgan, would be out of town on business for a week. Ironically, his victim was expected to arrive in Genoa that very same day. He immediately called his valet, John, and told him to rent a limousine and to put on his chauffeur's outfit. They then drove to the Genoa waterfront and waited next to the count's private slip.

The whole operation went smoothly. Bismarck forged the bank president's signature and presented the count with false American bonds worth five million American dollars. After the transaction was completed he immediately took a train to Geneva and converted the Count's European bonds to himself and transferred them to his own account. Bismarck was always careful not to bankrupt his conquests but he could not be aware that the count would eventually lose almost all of his assets later on with other poor investments.

Lisa finished her translation by adding, "I will personally see to it that my father receives his vendetta and that this cruel man is put in jail and reduced to poverty. I will do anything you ask of me, Mr. Nichols. This ingrate must be destroyed."

Pietro Columbo

"Thank you Countessa Lisa. That was a very interesting story. It was a typical sting operation by this cunning Bismarck. Believe me, Countessa, we will destroy him. Our next speaker will be Pietro Columbo.

Pietro was a well dress man of five foot nine and did not look the Mafia type. He could easily pass himself off as an executor of a major corporation. Even his speech was eloquent and sounded as though he was from the Park Avenue class of Manhattan. He overcame his lower Manhattan street accent by educating himself and by listening to speeches made by Franklin Delano Roosevelt. He would imitate the way Roosevelt talked and if one didn't look directly at him when he spoke he would sound like the president.

Pietro was born in Sicily and came to America when he was twelve. He attended grade school but because of the language barrier he was always in fist fights. When he turned sixteen he quit school but taught himself to speak proper English by imitating Roosevelt, reading books and listening to different radio announcers.

Pietro first became involved with the Mafia when he turned eighteen and was a runner for a bookie establishment collecting bets on the horses. He was later given the job as enforcer for a loan shark Mafia Don on the Manhattan docks. His reputation soon became well known within the mob because he was very successful as a collector. He killed his first man when a powerful dock worker reneged on his loan payments and decided to fight it out with Pietro. Young Pietro was infuriated and hit the man with a tire iron repeatedly across his skull until he was dead.

It wasn't long after that that Pietro became recognized as a ruthless man and in no time he was promoted up in the Mafia organization. When he turned forty he became the Manhattan chief after he personally assassinated the previous chief. He is now in his fifties and the premier ruler of all of the New York

City Boroughs. When people first met Pietro they assumed that he was a gentle man from his appearance and mannerism, but those who know him feared him, for he was as ruthless as they came. He was especially known as a man who would always make good on his vendettas. Any man who crossed him was automatically a dead pigeon.

Pietro stood up in the meeting and after sipping a glass of Anisette he said, "Thank you Mr. Nichols. My story is a little different than what has happened to the rest of you. You see, Bismarck didn't Con me directly, but he stole five-million dollars worth of my property and I intend to get it back one way or another." He first acknowledged the beautiful contessa by saying, "*Si bella, Contessa.*" She shyly smiled back.

Pietro's story began in the lower east side of Manhattan where he did a fabulous business in drugs. He didn't call it drugs or cocaine at this meeting but referred to it as white flour. Everyone knew what he was referring to.

It seems that Bismarck was playing pool in Little Italy, in lower Manhattan trying to hustle a well known local pool shark and bookie runner, called Zito. Zito was a very large and overweight man carrying three hundreds pounds on his rather short body of five-foot-five inches. Because of his weight and height it didn't seem possible that he could even play pool, but that was his ace in the hole. When he wanted to hustle someone he would grunt and groan over the pool table like he was having a hard time making a shot. But when the big money was down he change his style of shooting and didn't hold the stick as a normal pool player would. He would hold the stick over his right shoulder like he was throwing a spear. He would crouch a little so that the stick became level with the table. In this way his grotesque body wouldn't get in the way of his shots and all of a sudden he became a deadly shooter.

Bismarck was not aware of Zito's capabilities. He was out to hustle a hustler and, as usual, he prepared to do his homework. He first attended some of Zito's games with one of his disguises on. He even played with some of the local players to pass the time. He was still trying to find Zito's weakness. One day Zito was hustling a guy from California and was going through his normal strategy of playing conventionally. Then when the big money was on the table Bismarck saw Zito change the grip on his personal stick. Zito then wiped the man out and collected ten thousand dollars. Bismarck was impressed but he now knows Zito's gimmick. He didn't know how anybody could shoot pool holding the stick that way, but it's not how one plays the game. Winning is the only thing that counts.

Bismarck followed Zito home after that match to a cold water flat which was only a block away from the pool hall. After Zito entered the building Bismarck went into the vestibule and noted the names on the letter boxes on the wall and the call buttons above the boxes of each tenant. He saw that Zito's name was on the first floor so he pressed the buttons of the upper apartments. In those cold water flats there was no intercom system and invariably some tenant would always buzz back to release the door lock and yell down to find out who it is rather than walk down five flights of stairs to answer the door.

Bismarck entered the hall but didn't answer the call. He went to the back door and out into the back yard. He began looking through each window of the ground floor apartment and finally saw him kissing a fat woman in his bedroom. Zito then sat on the bed and she took off his pants for him. When he laid down she began providing him with oral sex. Bismarck figured he would be tied up for a spell so he went around to the dining room window and saw that Zito had left his personal pool stick in a case on the table. Bismarck saw his chance and climbed into the room. He was prepared ahead of time so he opened Zito's case and unscrewed the forward end of the stick and replaced it with another. The replacement stick front end was untrue and would cause Zito to miss some of his shots. Bismarck then went back to his own apartment and waited for the next day. He had one hundred thousand dollars on him to cover any bets. Just in case there was any trouble he carried his favorite 38 caliber pistol in a holster in the back of his trousers. He was ready.

Bismarck showed up at the pool hall at seven o'clock that evening but this time with a different disguise. Instead of being a middle aged man he was now a man that appeared to be in his late thirties with a large mustache. He began by playing some of the locals and winning every time. He was boisterous and acted like a bragger making fun of the locals saying he could beat any wop in Little Italy. He also acted as though he was drunk. The local Italians were becoming indignant and one player threatened to punch him out but a mafia soldier, Marco, stopped him and instead challenged him to play straight pool for a thousand dollars. Bismarck accepted and easily won. Zito was sitting at a distant table intensely watching the games. Bismarck knew that Zito would not get into the game until the betting money reached at least the ten thousand dollar level.

"Does anyone else care to lose their money?" Bismarck announced with a grin on his face after he won the game.

Marco was not through, yet. He raised the anti to five thousand dollars. By now everyone at the bar moved over to the center table to watch the match. They all knew that if Marco lost again this jerk would never see tomorrow. He doesn't like being a loser. Marco had the first shot and almost ran the table but missed his last shot. Bismarck then sunk the ball and proceeded to run the next four racks until he had fifty balls to his credit. After the match was over Marco said he didn't have five thousand on him. He only had one thousand dollars so he said he would have to accept his marker. Marco then wanted to play him again double or nothing.

Bismarck said, "If you don't have the cash on you you're out. I don't play against markers."

Bismarck then pulled out a roll of thousand dollar bills purposely to attract attention. Zito then stood up. He was impressed with the cash this guy was carrying so he walked over to the table.

He said, "I'll play you for ten thousand, punk." Zito figured he had better get some of that cash before Marco rolled him later on out in the street.

"You're on," responded Bismarck.

The game began and Bismarck noted that Zito was holding the stick normally. He figured that Zito was setting him up for the big kill and allow him win the first game which he did.

"If your think you are that good why don't we play for some real money," said Zito.

"What kind of money are you talking about?" asked Bismarck.

"Let's bet that whole roll you were flashing."

"It's a hundred grand... Okay. You going to match me or are you another poor slob who uses markers? I don't play against markers."

"Come with me over to the men's room, sucker," said Zito.

Bismarck was a bit leery about following him. He was ready to pull out his pistol if necessary but inside the men's room Zito produced a large cellophane package containing cocaine and said it was worth five million bucks on the streets.

"I'll bet this whole package against your one-hundred grand."

Bismarck then took out his pen knife and cut a small slit in the package. He tasted the product and decided it was the real McCoy. He agreed with the bet. Zito wasn't worried about losing the cocaine because he knew he could beat this man, and if he did lose Marco would see to it that it would be returned to him later.

Before the game began, Zito claimed that he was entitled to shoot first since he had lost the first game and that they will play the best two out of three games. Bismarck agreed and the contest was on. This time Zito held the stick like a spear so Bismarck knew he was serious.

Zito was able to run the first ten balls but missed the eleventh. He couldn't understand how he missed. The rest of the crowd was astonished at that miss. They knew he was a deadly shot and could make that shot with his eyes closed. Zito began sweating. Bismarck then proceeded to run the table and the next four racks without a miss. He won the next game just as easily and never gave Zito another turn. Zito then walked over to him and gave Bismarck the package and at the same time he looked over and nodded to Marco who got the message.

"By the way, what's your name?" asked Zito.

"Some people call me Bismarck."

Zito knew then that he had been taken. He had heard of the famous Bismarck Jones before, but had never met him personally.

"Thank you for your contribution. I'll be back tomorrow in

case anyone else wants to contribute some more money," said the smiling Bismarck. He noticed that Marco and a couple of men left through the front door.

Bismarck then unscrewed his stick and place the two separated pieces into his personal case and headed for the door. When he entered the street a car quickly pulled up to the entrance of the pool hall and Bismarck immediately ran to it and jumped into the back and onto the floor. The driver was his valet, John Wilson. The car quickly sped away while Marco and his men were firing Tommy guns and pistols at them. The car was especially made with reenforced steel in the side doors and trunk door. It had bullet proof glass windows all around. From then on the underworld was on the lookout for him but were unable to locate him. A price was put on his head by Columbo for one hundred thousand dollars.

Zito explained to Pietro, his mafia chief, on how this hustler got away with five million dollars worth of cocaine. Pietro was furious, not so much for the money, but because he was taken and was made a fool of. No one takes from his people.

Pietro concluded his talk in the meeting by saying, "This man will be tracked down and eliminated as an example to others who wish to try the same thing. I must have my vendetta."

Mr. Nichols then stood up and said, "Thank you Pietro. He seems to be slicker than I thought."

Pietro replied, "Mr. Nichols. You must tell me where I can find this Bismarck Jones. I will deal with him right away and you will have your revenge."

"I know how you feel, sir, but if I told you where he is you will certainly eliminate him, but then how will these other people get their money back?"

"I understand Mr. Nichols. I'm a fair man and I will give you and your friends ample time to get to him, but after that he is mine." With that Pietro sat down and finished his anisette. He had no intentions of waiting for Nichols to play his games. He will deal with Bismarck the first chance he can.

"Our next speaker will be Max Keller."

"I'm sorry, Sir, but I refuse to talk about my case."

"Very well, Max. No one is forcing you or anyone else in

this room to speak about their experiences if they don't wish to do so."

Cathy Sullivan's

"Our next speaker will be Miss Catherine Sullivan from Ireland."

As Cathy Sullivan rose from her comfortable chair she unfolded her shapely legs and began fixing her dress in a very alluring manner. All of the men in the room were obviously observing her movements but Slick had to make another derogatory remark.

"Yeah, baby. Tell us how Bismarck made passionate love with you and how he conned you."

"That's enough Mr. Barnum! We will have no more of that, do you understand? Otherwise I must ask you to leave."

"Okay, Chief. It's your show."

"Thank you. Miss Sullivan, you may begin."

"It all began two years ago. I met Mr. Jones in Ireland at a ball given by my aunt, Mrs. McIntyre, who was a widow at the time after losing her husband two years before. The ball was for the purpose of introducing her new boyfriend, Mr. William Jones from America, to our relatives and her close friends. Mr. Jones was a fine looking middle aged man with distinguished grey hair and mustache. I was very happy that my aunt had found such a nice looking man and gentle beau. She was extremely happy and was now laughing again. When her husband died she went into a shell and was so depressed she had contemplated suicide. Then after she met Mr. Jones her whole life changed for the good. Even though I still hate Mr. Jones for swindling a large fortune out of my aunt, I will say the one good thing that came out of this scam was that he did save my aunts life and she is still doing fine to this day.

"After I arrived at the ball, my aunt introduced me to Mr. Jones. We talked a bit and he asked me to dance. I didn't think nothing of it at the time so I did dance with him. He was certainly a fine dancer, but then a peculiar thing happened. He began to hold me very close, too close. He was very strong and I could feel the muscles in his back and arms. At the time I didn't know what to make of it, but when we finished the dance he excused himself and told my aunt that he was feeling a little poorly and wanted to lie down for a moment. He went upstairs and disappeared into his room.

"Later on, a fine looking gentleman came down the same stairs and walked right up to me. He introduced himself as John Smith. He then asked me to dance. He was so attractive and persuasive I could hardy refuse him. When we began to dance I had a funny feeling that I knew him and if I closed my eyes I could swear that I was still dancing with Mr. Jones. At the time I didn't know what to make of it but I was enjoying myself so I never gave it another thought. After the dance he confessed to me that he had crashed the party just to meet me. He said he will have to leave the party before he is caught but he would contact me next weekend. He left through the front door, just like that he was gone. I thought I would never see him again but of course I did, many times.

"Even after he left he still reminded me of Mr. Jones, but Mr. Jones had brown eyes and Mr. Smith had those pretty blue eyes. It was so confusing to me at the time. A half hour later Mr. Jones reappeared but he never asked me to dance again. He spent the rest of the evening with my aunt telling her funny stories and she would laugh out loud. She was so happy. I was pleased for her.

"The next weekend Mr. Smith presented himself at my front door. I was upstairs in my room when our butler called me on our intercom and said a gentleman wishes to speak with me. I went down to the living room and there he was. He was such a gorgeous man. I knew I had falling in love with him the minute I met him and now I was sure of it. I felt like I was a teenager again being courted by the captain of our school soccer team. He asked me if I would like to take a drive in his new Jaguar, and I accepted. We drove through the woods and up to Blarney hill which was sometimes called lovers hill. We talked and talked and then he kissed me. I didn't refuse him. To tell you the truth, I rather encouraged it.

"Well, one thing led to another and before we knew it we became serious lovers. I would meet him only on weekends at

Flanigan's hotel on the beach which was about an hours drive from my home. My mom would kid me and say, `Going to visit your prince charming again my dear. The way you two are going about it he had better ask you to marry him pretty soon or it could be decided by a shot gun. Your father is very disturbed about these secret meetings.'

"I said to my mother, `Don't be too hasty. I'm sure he loves me as I do him. Give him a little time. It was only a month since I met him and you know how these Americans are. They want to try out the merchandise before they buy it.'

"She said, `Yes my dear but it seems to me you are letting him wear the merchandise a little too often.'" Some of the male guests laughed.

She continued being very open and frank. "I said, `But mom, it's not that I'm a virgin. I was married before and after being disappointed in that marital relationships, I really wanted to try out the merchandise myself ahead of time and to be sure I was not disappointed again. I don't mind admitting that the merchandise fits very well.' My first husband, you see, was killed falling off a horse and was impotent. So I didn't really miss him.

"She said, `Shame on you, daughter, to admit that you are enjoying this kind of a relationship. You should go to church and pray to God for forgiveness.'

"Our love affair went on for the next six months. He seemed to be very rich and took me to all of the exclusive and expensive restaurants. We were very happy, but I was beginning to wonder why he hadn't propose to me. Then all of a sudden he disappeared. I thought it was just a coincidence but Mr. Jones had also disappeared at the same time. I discovered later that my aunt was defrauded out of a two hundred thousand pounds by this Mr. Jones and neither she nor I have ever seen or heard from either of them again.

"When you wrote that letter to my aunt I decided to follow it up myself since my aunt isn't feeling well after Mr. Jones had left her. I was also hoping that I might find my Mr. Smith in the process. I always had a suspicion that Mr. Smith and Mr. Jones were partners together in this swindle like a father and son act, and I still feel that if I find one I will find the other. You see, I'm still in love with Mr. Smith and I do want to marry him if he will still have me."

"Thank you, Miss Sullivan. Before this evening is over I'm sure you will be surprised at the true identities of Mr. Jones and Mr. Smith. We will see to it that your aunt will have her revenge but as far as marrying Mr. Smith is concerned, that's another matter."

Miss Sullivan was a bit disappointed at his remarks and sat down. Mr. Nichols then asked everyone to take a ten minute break.

Slick Barny

When they were all assembled again Mr. Nichols introduced the next guest speaker. "Our next speaker will be Mr. James Barnum from Brooklyn, better known as Slick Barny. Mr. Barnum, you're on."

Slick Barny was rather slim at five foot eleven and weighed in at one hundred and forty pounds. He was in his forties but had prematurely lost a good deal of his black hair. He seemed to always have a cigarette in his mouth. When he stood up he tried to give the impression that he was a tough man and spoke with a Brooklyn accent. He was not clean shaven which hid a scare on his left cheek.

"Yeah. Tanks. You know, I'm a pretty popular guy in the Williamsburg section of Brooklyn. I don't even mind admitting I'm a hustler in the pool hall, but I never conned anyone. I'm not a crook like this clown, Bismarck. I don't go around stealing money from little old ladies, either. To me that's the lowest form of a human being there is, see.

"I don't mind losing to another hustler, but what this guy did to me was outright stealing. Like I said, everyone knows me in my section of Brooklyn because I was always in the big bucks. I was also very generous with hand outs to the locals. I grew up in a tough neighborhood and everyone knew me before when my parents were poor people. When I made it big it was nothing for me to hand out ten or twenty bucks to some poor old lady in the community. They would always say to me, `God bless you Slick. You should be a saint.'

"Anyways, one day I was at Harry's pool hall making small bets when in comes this old dude carrying a pool stick case. He challenged the winner in the game that was in process by putting fifty cents on the end of the table. That's the way it's done. You're king of the hill, as long as you continue to win. The table is yours and everyone else has to challenge you. Well, in no time this dude was hogging the table. He couldn't lose. The bets were too small for me to enter so I watched a little longer.

"Pretty soon another hustler, the Cat, comes into the pool hall. I knew him from previous matches I had with him. He was good but I could take him anytime. When he passed me by he gave me that certain look and I shrugged my shoulder which meant, `I'm not in the game so go ahead and hustle this dude.' He then put a buck on the end of the table to be next. After the dude won the game the Cat pulled out one hundred bucks and laid it on the table. The dude accepted the challenge and in no time at all the dude beat the Cat again. He ran the table four times.

"The Cat then said,`Let's make it double or nothing,' and he lost again. This time the Cat said, `Let's make it for a thousand smackers.'

"Now it's starting to get interesting. I knew that the Cat was setting him up for the big kill working the bet up to the twenty thousand category. That amount was the Cat's limit. Sure enough this dude eventually won all the matches up to the twenty grand bet and now the big money was being played. The Cat looked at me and smiled. He had set this patsy up for the kill. This time the game was rough. The Cat was playing very cautious not giving his opponent a clear shot whenever he was stuck himself. This went on for awhile for six racks but then the door was open. The Cat made a bad shot and the dude ran the rest of that table and the following two tables to win all the money.

"That's when I got into the picture. I put a fifty cent piece on the end of the pool table. The dude looked right into my eyes and stared at me for the longest time. It was a weird feeling. I thought he was trying to intimidate me, but I've been around, see. I'm not afraid of anyone.

"I challenged him right off with twenty grand. He agreed and the game began. It was a battle and several times I thought I would lose but I eventually won. He then quit and left the pool hall. It was kind of an odd thing to do, but then I figured he knew he met his master. I took the money and did what I always do with my winnings. I put them in a canvas bag that I always carried around with me. I never worried about anyone stealing from me because everyone was afraid of me. They all knew that they would be dead meat if they tried. One time an out-of-towner tried it. He was found lying in the east river the next day, dead as a door nail. Nobody messes with me, see. I guarantee that they don't.

"That evening I called one of the local girls to have a spaghetti diner with me at Pasta Mia's restaurant. I never had any trouble getting dates. It was kind of an honor for a girl to go out with me. Naturally, I made love with them that night just to make them happy. I rarely went out with the same girl twice. Sometimes I would take on married broads during the day when their husbands were working. I tried to please them all. Some of the girls were older and some might even be considered jail bait. I didn't care who I screwed, see.

"I had previously picked up this Italian girl, Angela, at the news stand. Her father didn't approve of her dating me, so we met a couple of blocks away from her home. I got out of the car to open the car door for her on the passenger side when this son-of-bitching dude puts a gun in my ribs. He removed my own gun from its holster and we all got into the car. He sat in the back and told me to drive away. When we got to an isolated area under the Williamsburg bridge he told me to stop and we both should get out. He then drove away and left us stranded there. He got away with my canvas bag containing about three hundred grand in it, the bastard.

"I never found out who he was until I received your letter, Mr. Nichols. So you see, not only is Pietro out to get his hide, I also want a piece of it myself, but not until I get my money back. What I want to know now, Mr. Nichols, is this Bismarck guy my dude?"

"Thank you for your story. Yes Mr. Barnum, he is your dude. It seems that Bismarck will stoop to any level to make a buck. He's not only a hustler, a gambler, and a confidence man but now I see he's an out and out crook. Interesting."

Angela Wagner's Minister

"Now we shall hear from Angela Wagner from Ohio," announced Mr. Nichols.

Miss Wagner was a forty-five year old spinster who had inherited a fortune from her parents when they were both killed in an auto accident. She lives in an old but rich section in the suburbs of Cleveland. Her worth was estimated in the millions but she lived rather simple. She never learned to drive and was completely dependent on her chauffeur to drive her around. She rarely left the house except on Sundays when she attended the Community Methodist Church. The only other servants that were employed by her were a maid and a cook but no butler. The maid also acted as the butler.

Miss Wagner was still attractive in her own way but she was considered an introvert. She wouldn't even attend any of the social parties given by the exclusive upper class in her town. She was tall at five foot seven with long brown hair that was always tied in a bun. She always wore loose old fashion dresses that hid her rather large breasts. She was a little ashamed of her bust size and would hunch herself over so that they would not protrude so much. This made her appear round shouldered in public.

One day the old pastor of the church had a heart attack and died. He was replaced by a much younger Reverend Jones who appeared to be in his forties. Reverend Jones was a delight to the community and made Sunday sermons more enjoyable. Since his arrival Miss Wagner began attending church functions as well. She sort of had a crush on the new minister who was very handsome and, more important, not married. He was always paying her pleasant complements whenever he met her.

He would say to her, "Miss Wagner, you look exceptional attractive this morning," or, "I love your dress, Miss Wagner."

She would smile at his compliments and blushed a little. He made her feel young again. She was not used to this attention and when she was alone in her home she began having naughty thoughts about him. She envisioned herself alone with him in her bed, both naked making violent love. This had never happened to her before. She always had control her emotions especially when it came to the opposite sex. This man was affecting her differently.

One Sunday afternoon, after church, Reverend Jones was standing at the exit of the church saying goodby to the parishioners as he always did. The last person to come out was Miss Wagner. She planned it that way. Even she didn't know what had come over her when she invited him to have dinner with her that evening. He, of course, accepted.

The minister later drove up to a large mansion that was located at the edge of town. Miss Wagner's father had the mansion built on at this particular sight to be away from the average town folks but still close enough to have control his employees that worked in his factory. The mansion was fifty years old and was a replica of an estate in Germany. He arrived from Germany with his poor immigrant family and became rich in textiles. He had always admired the German mansion when he was young boy and when he had the finances he built his home exactly like it. He had to go back to Germany to acquire the original plans. Her mother was American born of English extraction.

When the minister arrived she met him at the door. This time she wasn't wearing her normal dreary dress, but was now in an alluring evening gown that she had purchase the week before. This time she didn't particularly try to hide her large bosom, either. One might even say she was a little over exposed. Her long brown hair was now combed straight down below her shoulders. She definitely could pass for a different woman. A very sensual woman, indeed.

The reverend was fascinated with her new appearance and smiled at her, "Miss Wagner, you are the most attractive woman in this whole parish." He couldn't help but glance down at the creamy mounds formed by the upper curvature of her white soft bosom.

"Thank you very much, Reverend. Please come in." She knew she had impressed him and smiled to herself.

During dinner she said to him, "Reverend Jones, I must say that ever since you took over, the church is now a very pleasant experience. Your sermons are most interesting, and so modern in comparison to our past minister. He was so drab and old fashion he was losing all of the young people. Since you have arrived six months ago, things have changed tremendously. Everyone tells me that they now look forward to our Sunday meetings. The young are starting to come back and are becoming more involved in church affairs again. It's wonderful."

"I thank you for that, Miss Wagner. When I preached my first sermon here the church was half empty. I knew I had to do something, and thanks to you and all the other parishioners, we now have a full church every Sunday with loving people who truly care for our Lord. Love, Miss Wagner, is the key to everything. It is the love of God and the love we have for each other that makes this a happy world and a better place to live." He then stood up and received her hand. They both went into the living room holding hands.

Miss Wagner melted every time he said the word love and was now very uncomfortable holding his hand. She then excused herself and went up to the ladies room on the second floor. She was definitely having a rough time of it and was now experiencing sensations she hadn't had since she was a teenager. She washed her face with cold water and then starred at herself in the mirror. Her face was red from blushing. When she felt better she came down to her guest again who was sitting on the couch having a cold lemonade.

"I'm sorry to leave you alone so long, Reverend. How is your lemonade?"

"Fine. You know, Miss Wagner, I have been noticing you in church and at our functions off and on now for the past six months and I must admit, if you will pardon me for being so forward, I'm rather attracted to you. May I visit with you more often, privately I mean."

"Reverend Jones... I don't know what to say." She quickly stood up and began walking around the living room floor. "Are you serious, Reverend?"

"Yes I am, Miss Wagner. You see it has been a long struggle

for me in this profession. I spent most of my early years on location in South America helping those poor souls down there and spreading the word of our lord. I never had much time to consider the opposite sex or, for that matter, matrimony. Now that I have my own Parish and a steady income I think it is time that I settled down and began a family of my own. When I met you, I have to confess, I was very impressed and I said to myself, I think I have found the right lady. Miss Wagner, I would like to see you more often and hope that some day you will feel the same way about me."

"My goodness, Reverend. I don't know what to say. I must admit that I am also attracted to you and I would like to see you more often myself, I suppose."

The minister stood up and took her hand and bent over and kissed it. He then said, "Thank you, Miss Wagner. You don't know how much this means to me and I promise to be a gentleman at all times. But please, Miss Wagner, when we are alone and not in church please call me William?"

"I will, if you will call me Angela."

They both agreed and he finally excused himself because he said he had to run an errand. He thanked her for dinner and as they approached the door he made an unusual move. He turned around to face her and then put his arms around her and slowly placed a tender kiss on her lips. She didn't stop him either. As he went out the door she clasped her mouth with her left hand to capture the sensation of his kiss.

Her maid then walked over to her and said, "He is sure a fine looking gentleman, Miss. I think he likes you very much. That dress we selected I'm sure had a lot to do with it."

Angela was still looking out toward the driveway and said, "I hope you're right, Estell. Thank you for helping me select this dress. I thought it was a bit much but I think it helped. He couldn't keep his eyes off of me. I have to admit, I'm also very fond of him."

Reverend Jones began seeing Angela quite frequently after that. The reverend was very careful not to get over rambunctious, but even he had his limits. She was a very attractive lady and he now wanted her badly. After two weeks of seeing her almost everyday the reverend began getting more familiar with her. One evening, when the maid and the cook were off duty, they were both sitting on the couch having port wine together. After they finished one glass the reverend poured her another, and later another. When the reverend saw that she was becoming very relaxed he kissed her ever so gently. She responded very well so he kissed her more, but this time he was a little more aggressive. He placed his hand over her breast but she slowly pulled it away.

"My dear. I love you so much I can't stand to be away from you, even for one day." He then put his hand on her breast again. This time she didn't remove it.

"I feel the same way, William. What are we going to do?"

He continued to fondle her and finally she opened her mouth to accept him. He then put his hand inside of her dress and caressed her bare breast touching her nipple. He lowered his other hand down to her womb and began rubbing her.

"I love you, Angela. Please, can't we go to bed?"

"I don't know, William. Maybe people will talk."

"Let them talk. I want to marry you. I want the whole world to know I love you. Please Angela. I'm so frustrated I need you badly."

"Alright, William. If you think it's the right thing to do."

Angela was no virgin. She was actually molested by her father's cousin when she was sixteen. He continued to rape her several months after that until one day she couldn't stand it any longer and shot him dead with her fathers pistol which he kept in a night table in his bedroom. There was a major scandal over this incident but she was later acquitted for justifiable homicide. Because of her bad experience with her cousin, Angela would not let another man touch her, not even her father. She withdrew from society for many years and consoled herself in prayers at her church for forgiveness over killing a man.

Reverend Jones was a professional at alluring women. He made her forget about the past and broke her hatred for men. He slowly made her feel like she was a desirable woman again. She was now willing to try making love but this time it would be with someone she cared for. The reverend, of course, knew about her past so he was prepared to take his time in this courtship.

They went upstairs and into her bedroom holding hands. She undressed in the closet and later come out with a black negligee on. She had a fine figure and her large bosom seemed ready to pop out of the thin cloth that barely covered her nipples. He was very excited by now and was almost undressed himself except for his shorts. He observe her sensual motion as she approached him. He couldn't wait any longer. He put his arms around her and began kissing her again and again. He then removed her negligee and his own shorts. Jones slowly moved her towards the bed and lifted her on to the mattress. He place his head between the channel of her two large breasts and began sucking them one at a time. He finally mounted her and they began their intercourse. After ten minutes of a passionate love they both reached ecstacy and she screamed out loud while he was yelling for joy. When it was all over she began crying. She had never experienced this wonderful feeling of a climax before even when she was raped by her father's cousin. She finally told him about her ordeal with her second cousin. He acted as though he didn't know anything about it, but he said he understood the humiliation she must have gone through over these past years. He consoled her and said that it didn't make any difference to him about her past because he loved her with all his heart. She was so happy now and truly in love with this wonderful man.

Over the following weeks the reverend kept delaying the date of their marriage. He would find all kinds of excuses until one day he said to her, "Angela, we can't live in your home as husband and wife. This is a mansion. It just doesn't look right that a minister should be married to a millionaires living so luxuriously. First of all, look at our church. It's run down and the minister's home is small and not really suitable to raise a family. You are used to fine things and a beautiful home. I could never give you that on my income."

"But William. I love you so much, I would be willing to live with you anywhere," Angela pleaded.

"I know you would, dearest, but don't you see we really need a new and mutual home. The church also should be enlarged to meet the needs of the congregation. The parishioners are growing so rapidly that we can't possibly have a prayer meeting with everyone in it. What I'm asking is that we should expand our church and build a new ministers home. That way, we will be closer to our worshipers and everyone could see that our marriage and the church go together."

"How will you pay for this expansion, William?"

"Well, I was thinking that if you sold your home you should be able to donate a good portion for this endeavor without hurting your assets, and with you in the lead I'm sure that the other parishioners would match or even double your donation."

Angela thought about it for a while and finally said, "How much would you need for this enterprise?"

"I would say a total of a million dollars would be sufficient to cover all of the expenses. If this task could be accomplished I would more than happy to marry you and we could raise a fine religious family."

"Well, I absolutely will not sell my home, at least not at the present time, but I could donate say $500,000 in cash and I'm sure I could get the rest of the parish to match it. Would that be satisfactory, William?"

"It sure would. And, of course, since you are the prime benefactor I want you to handle all the financial details for this project. Would you do that, my dear? And when the work is all done you and I will be the first couple to be married in the newly renovated church. I will ask the Bishop to perform the ceremony"

"It would be wonderful, William. I agree to your terms."

The project began one month after the parish had matched Angela's donation. The reverend hired a contractor to do the construction who showed up with ten men with bull dozers and dump trucks. They first had to tear down the old ministers home and then they began digging a huge hole in its place for the foundation.

Later in the week the reverend went over to Angela's home and said he would need five hundred thousand in advance to buy all the material needed for the structure. She made out a check to him for that amount without hesitation. As the foundation walls were being poured with concrete the reverend then asked Angela for another three hundred thousand dollars in advance to renovate the church. She again gave him the money unquestioned.

That weekend Reverend Jones told Angela that he had to go to New York for a minister's meeting and he would be back that Monday. Unfortunately, he never returned and the workers also disappeared. She and her parish friends were jilted out of eight hundred thousand dollars. The minister and none of the contractors were ever found by the police. Out of the eight hundred thousand, the reverend had to give the false contractor one hundred thousand dollars in cash. When Angela finished her story she sat down sobbing.

"That was a very interesting story, Miss Wagner," said Mr. Nichols.

"What I would like to know, Mr. Nichols, is my reverend this Bismarck Jones you all are referring to?" ask Angela.

"I'm afraid so, Miss Wagner."

"But you must understand one thing, I still love him and want him back. He's the only man that has ever made me feel like a woman again and if you will tell me where he is I will forgive him for whatever he did. After all, he only took eight hundred thousand dollars, which is an insignificant amount for me. I just want him back."

"I'm sorry, Miss Wagner. But I'm afraid you would have to share this man with a dozen other women. It just wouldn't work."

She sat down again feeling dejected and helpless as she stared at the ground not saying another word.

Mrs. Mary Elsworth

"Thank you Miss Wagner for your story, and now we will hear from Mrs. Mary Elsworth."

Mrs. Elsworth was not a pretty woman and might be considered a little homely. She was fifty-five years old and many thought she was much older. She was extremely overweight and very short at five foot even. After her husband died she was not the least bit interested in meeting another man. Her garment business in Liverpool, England kept her very busy. By the end of the day she was exhausted from working with all that excessive weight and was glad to go home and just rest.

One day she was dealing with a male buyer from New York who was interested in purchasing a line of her dresses. The buyer introduced himself as William Jones who represents Macy's department store.

"Mrs. Elsworth, in New York we heard so much about your marvelous collection of women's dresses and I have been assigned to look into your stock. Yesterday, I attended the London fashion show and when I saw your new series of dresses being modeled I was completely impressed. What I liked about your style of clothes is that it looks more American than European. Even though the French dresses are popular in Europe they do not sell very well in America.

"Mrs. Elsworth, before I place an order with you I would like to discuss some further details with you over dinner tonight. It's been a long trip for me and I would like to relax a little with an attractive lady. This is only my second night in England and I still haven't had a chance to dined out at one of your exclusive restaurants. I'm a widower myself and all alone. Please, would you do me the honor of having dinner with me and to show me the ropes, so to speak?"

"I don't know, Mr. Jones. I usually dine alone at home and it's been a long while since I attended any of our fine restaurants. You see, my husband was not well for many years and we sort of stopped going out for dinner."

"I'm sorry for your loss. I can sympathize with you since I also lost a very dear and loving wife. It also has been very difficult for me."

"Well, seeing that you are alone here I suppose I could accompany you just for this evening and this way I may be able to answer some of your questions about our business."

"Good. Then I shall pick you up at seven this evening. Is that satisfactory, Mrs. Elsworth?"

"Yes. That would be just fine."

Bismarck later that evening picked her up with a rented limousine. They were driven to an exclusive restaurant, called the Astor House. Bismarck was formally dressed in a black tuxedo and Mrs. Elsworth was dressed in one her special evening gowns which she designed herself. Bismarck remarked to her how lovely she looked but the truth of the matter is no evening gown could have improve her appearance. She was just too large. When she was seated the chair simply disappeared from under her. Bismarck felt a little uneasy escorting her but business is business. One has to make certain sacrifices if one wants to be a successful confidence man.

"Oh, this is a lovely place, Mr. Jones. I'm glad you invited me."

"Mrs. Elsworth. Could we be less formal. Please call me William?"

"Very well, William. Then you must call me Mary."

"Good. Now may I order you a cocktail, Mary?"

"Thank you. I'll have whatever you are having, William."

Bismarck ordered two Martinis and told the waiter to later bring a bottle of Champagne. He was avoiding asking her to dance because he thought it would be a major chore dragging her around the floor. He was a little embarrassed at the thought of appearing comical in front of the other patrons. He finally got up enough courage to ask her and to his dismay she readily accepted. As they began dancing, to his surprise, she carried herself very well on the floor and he began feeling better about the whole affair.

Back at the table she asked, "William, what details about my business did you wish to discuss, this evening?"

"Oh, that can wait. I'm having such a good time, who can discuss business now."

She giggled and raised her glass and said, "Touche." Bismarck ordered a second bottle of Champaign but instead of her getting more mellow as he had planned, he was the one that was feeling tipsy with the drinks. The third bottle did him in and he passed out in his chair. The next morning he woke up in a strange bedroom naked under the sheets. A few minutes later Mary walked in with a tray of food and her own recipe for a hangover.

"Now you drink this. I guarantee it will get rid of your hangover in no time at all."

It looked like tomato juice mixed with orange juice but he drank it anyway. Sure enough he began feeling better and was now getting hungry.

"Who removed my cloths, Mary?"

"I did, love. You needn't be so shy. I've seen naked men before. I must say, you don't have the body of a man in his sixties. You must keep yourself in wonderful shape."

"Tell me, Mary. What happened here last night?"

"Don't you remember? We made passionate love, my sweet. I haven't had sex like that since I was a young girl fooling around with our gardener. My husband was a poor lover but I loved him very much and I accepted my role as a caring wife. But now that I have found you I feel like a new woman again. Now you rest a little and later we will carry on where we left off last night." She then leaned over and kissed him on the lips.

After she left, Bismarck couldn't believe what she just said. He didn't remember having sex with anyone but in his dreams he did. He remembered making love with a beautiful blonde in her twenties. All he could say was, "Oh my God, what did I do?"

Three hours later Mary popped in again but this time she was dressed in a huge negligee. When Bismarck looked at her he almost vomited. She then took off her negligee all he could see was rolling flab. She then crawled in bed with him and without a word she practically picked him up and place him on top of her. Bismarck felt helpless. He was now engulfed in a giant pillow of soft flesh. She reach down and inserted his penis into her. Bismarck wasn't sure he had even entered her because there was so much meat. She proceeded to lift him in the air in an up and down motion and in no time she reached her own climax. To his surprise he also climaxed. She then tossed him over to the other side of the bed and left. He promptly fell asleep again still not feeling very well.

That evening she was back with dinner but first they went through the whole love making routine again. Bismarck had never experienced this helplessness of being raped before, but now he knows the feeling. She again left him to finish his dinner. He decided he has to get out of here or go bananas. He dressed and tried to open the door. It was locked. He finally realized he was her prisoner. He decided to pick the lock but found the door was secured with an iron bar across the other side of the door and was locked. He looked to escape through the bedroom window but it had bars.

"What's going on here?" he said to himself.

At 10 P.M. she showed up again. "How are you doing, lover?"

"Am I your prisoner?" he asked.

"I'm afraid you are, my sweet. I haven't had the joy and thrills of sex with a good man for a long time. It's not easy for a woman of my size to latch on to a good looking man such as yourself. You're a wonderful lover. I'm sorry, William, but I cannot permit you to leave. Now that I've found you, you will be mine as long as I need you."

With that she started to remove her clothes again. Bismarck never hit a woman before but this was a desperate situation. When she came close to him he simply pushed her hard and she fell to the floor. She screamed for her butler who was a huge man and also her enforcer. Bismarck headed out the door but he was intercepted by the butler who grabbed him. Bismarck was having trouble with this man because he was so strong. He had Bismarck in a bear hug and held him tight. Finally Bismarck was able to kick him below the belt with his knee and the butler released his grip just long enough for Bismarck to throw a punch. The man went down and Bismarck ran out the door and out into the street. He was free. This was the first time that Bismarck lost a scam and was happy to do so. He never returned to Liverpool again. This was the worst experience he had ever encountered in all his years as a Con man.

Mr. Nichols then said to Mrs. Elsworth, "Well, it seems that our Bismarck isn't the perfect confidence man we thought he was. He did have a weakness, after all. So before he could extort any money out of you, Mrs. Elsworth, he ran out on you. Fascinating."

"I didn't know he was trying to extort money from me, Mr. Nichols. He can have whatever he wants as long as he comes back to me. I still want him. My life has not been the same since he left me. Please, Mr. Nichols. Tell me where he is. I'll pay whatever you ask."

"I'm sorry, Mrs. Elsworth. I just can't do that. There are others here to consider."

She began screaming at him. She demanded his address and then began pushing him around. Finally, Mr. Nichols called to Wilson to throw her out. It took him and two other men to get her out the front door and off the premises.

When John returned Mr. Nichols asked him, "How come we invited her if she wasn't a victim of Bismarck's."

"All I know is when Bismarck returned from that caper I had asked him how it went. He simply said that it was a very successful enterprise so I assumed he was able to extort money out of her. That's why I put her name on the list of victims. I can see now he was probably ashamed of what happened and didn't want to admit that he lost his first scam over a fat old broad."

Mr. Nichols had a grin on his face and said, "When we finish breaking him, I will have the greatest pleasure of reminding him of that experience. His reaction should be very interesting. I might even turn him over to her as his final punishment. He would be her prisoner and lover for the rest of his unscrupulous life." They all began laughing.

Edward Young's Loan

After Mrs. Elsworth was escorted out Mr. Nichols addressed the remaining group and said, "Now we have two unusual but similar cases. I would like to introduce you to Mr. Edward Young from Australia, and a Mr. John Watts from San Francisco. Which one of you would care to start?" Mr. Young stood up and asked to speak first.

Mr. Young was a very successful rancher of beef and sheep in Australia. He was a hard working man who was now in his fifties. He was proud of his ancestral background when he discovered his grandparents came from the jails of London in the nineteenth century and served out their prison time as farm workers. He was a rugged man at six foot three and could handle himself in any bar room brawl. He wore a large ten gallon hat and a tan buckskin jacket. He could easily pass for an American cowboy. He was married and had three children, a boy and two girls.

"I'm pleased to be able to tell you my story on how I was duped out of my money by this contemptible man. It all started a couple of years ago when I came to America looking for business investments. One day, when I was reading the Los Angeles Times newspaper, I came across an advertisement from a loan company that would give loans of one hundred thousand dollars or more. The advertisement said that the Security Loan Company will provide low rate loans with reasonable payments that may be spread over a twenty year period. It advertised that an easy loan may be awarded with a small deposit at a eight percent interest rate. The address of the loan company was on Wilshire Boulevard in the middle of a mall where there were many business offices. Being from out of town I thought that this would help me since most of my capital was still in Australia and was tied up in my ranch and other properties.

"I went to that office and was greeted by a most beautiful blond at the front desk of the Security Loan office. She asked me a few questions and then introduced me to a Dr. William Jones, the president of the loan company. He was a man in his fifties and spoke eloquently. He was very business like. I told him I wanted to borrow five hundred thousand dollars which I will use to buy some property in San Fernando, California.

"He said, `That's no problem, Mr. Young. What we will do is make a financial and character reference check on you first to insure that you are a safe investor and after that is accomplished you will be required to deposit up front twenty percent of your loan. I know it sounds rather high but this deposit is only temporary and it will be held by our firm for only a year. When we see that you are making your payments on time and your business is doing well this money will be returned to you in full. We only do this for our protection as well as yours. If, for some reason, you can't make a payment within the year we will simply deduct that amount out of your deposit. This will then give you extra time and protection in case your business deals aren't running smoothly and in this way no one gets hurt. Is that agreeable to you, Mr. Young?'

"I told him it was a satisfactory arrangement.

"Then he said. `In the meantime, while you are waiting to have your references cleared why don't you allow my secretary, Miss Lovelady, escort you around Los Angeles at my expense. There is so much to see here in L.A. and Miss Lovelady is just the right person to do it. I expect your clearance should only take only a couple of days.'

"Well, how could I not accept such a wonderful gesture from him. Miss Lovelady was extremely pretty and was very well endowed, if you know what I mean.

"That evening Miss Lovelady (Janet) took me to a marvelous nightclub and we had such a wonderful time with a fine dinner and an outstanding American band. She then took me to her apartment and before I knew it we were in bed together. She specialized in unusual sex and I must admit it was most enjoyable. I confess of being a married man but Janet was so very attractive that I just couldn't resist myself. It was a wonderful experience.

"The next morning Dr. Jones called me at her apartment and

said that my references passed with no problems, and if I would come to his office and deposit the required one hundred thousand dollars he could start the necessary paper work to grant me the loan. I did go back to his firm with Janet and I made out a check to cover the deposit. Janet said she had work to do and that I should come by her apartment later that evening because she was preparing a special dinner for me. That evening I did go to her apartment and every evening after that for the next week. It was a wonderful. Making love with her was getting to me. I was beginning to fall in love with her. I was having a difficult time of it because I still loved my wife and children back in Australia. I was ashamed of myself but I lost all control of my emotions over this woman. I became completely addicted with her.

"The following Monday evening I went to her apartment as usual to take her out to dinner and when I knocked on the door no one answered. I knocked several more times with no response. Finally her next door neighbor answered and she said that Miss Lovelady is no longer at this address. I asked her if she left a forwarding address and she said she didn't and that maybe the manager could help. When I went to see the manager he was somewhat surprised because he was never informed that she would leave so soon, especially since she paid her rent six months in advance. I then took a cab to the Security Loan's office and when I got there the place was completely empty. I finally called the police and all they could say was that I was taken by a Con artist and they will try to locate this Dr. Jones for me but they didn't have much hope of finding him. That crook took me for one hundred thousand dollars. Now that I am listening to all of the stories from your other guests I can only assume that my Dr. Jones was also this Bismarck chap. Am I correct?"

After hearing Mr. Young's story, Mr. Nichols had a small grin on his face and was shaken his head. The more stories he heard the more fascinating he became over Bismarck's accomplishments.

"Yes, I'm sure he is our Bismarck. Not only is he a crook but now I see he is an extortionist. Our next speaker is from Mr. Watts from San Francisco."

Mr. Watts stood up and said, "Ladies and gentleman. My case is very similar to Mr. Young's except that my deposit was considerably more and my escort was a red head. Mr. Young, did your Janet have a red rose tattooed on her hip, by any chance?"

"Yes. As a matter of fact she did. I told the police that and they said she was probably Mary Allen, a well known hooker who was last seen walking the streets in New York."

"Well, it seems your Janet, my Louise, and this hooker Mary Allen are one in same but each with different colored hair. When you mentioned her expertise, I knew there was some sort of a connection. It seems, Dr. Jones used the same extortion act on me as well, Mr. Nichols, except he manage to extract two hundred thousand dollars out of me. I won't go into the details of my losses because my experience is very similar to Mr. Young's, except it happened in San Francisco."

"Thank you Mr. Watts for your information. And now Mr. and Mrs. Schwartz, you're next."

"No thank you. We would prefer not to comment. These stories are very interesting, I have to admit."

"Very well then. It seems that we have run out of story tellers and now that Mr. and Mrs. Schwartz refuse to discuss their losses with us, this phase of our business is concluded.

Charles Gridley

"What about my story?" There was a voice that came from a gentleman sitting in the back of the room.

"Oh! And who might you be, sir?" said Mr. Nichols.

"I'm Charles Gridley from Montana. Everybody calls me Chuck. You didn't invite me, but I heard about this meeting through a friend of mine who happens to know Mr. Watts here. You see I have also been swindled by this Mr. Jones, at least I think it was him."

Charles Gridley was a true cowboy who was now in his seventies. At the turn of the century he was just a hired hand punching cattle. He originally came from Texas as a cow hand driving a large herd north that were to be sold to a New York investor who was expanding his assets in Montana. Gridley ended up marring the New Yorker's daughter and eventually he became one of the largest ranch owners in the country. They were unable to have children so in the event of his death his property would go to his brother's children living in Texas.

Gridley continued, "I'm a cattle man with one hundred thousand head of the finest herd in the country. I've worked hard all my life raising and selling these animals for beef and I have to admit business has been very profitable.

"Well, one day last year after I lost my wife I sat down and thought about my life in general. With all of the hard work I did over so many years I never took one solitary vacation. So I ups and heads for sunny Southern California. The weather was to my liking so I decided that I should buy a place to stay during the winter months.

"I went to a bar one evening near Rodeo Drive in Beverly Hills, where most of the Hollywood people shop, and struck up a conversation with an elderly gentleman whose name was Howard Jones. We got to talking and I casually mentioned that I was interesting in buying a spread here in Hollywood. Well, it was a down right coincidence because this here Jones feller happened to be selling his place in Beverly Hills. He even offered to drive me to it and show me the estate. I had nothing else to do so I went right along with him.

"The place was beautiful. It had everything that I wanted, a pool, a tennis court, and plenty of property so's I won't be looking in my neighbor's backyard. I fell in love with the property. I asked him what was the going price and he said two million dollars. Now I'm nobodies fool. I've been around and I know that a piece of property like this was worth a hell of a lot more than that. So I asked him why so cheap. He said he was in debt up to his ears and had to bail out fast.

"Well, we sat down at the dinning room table and we discussed it further. He had all the necessary papers right there on the table ready to do business. I told him that my accountant will have to go over these papers first before I can buy the place. He said he was sorry but he doesn't have the time to wait because he does have other offers. He may have to sell to one of them first and the only reason he hasn't sold it already was because that party was having some difficulty transferring their capital to cash for the down payment and it would take a few days. He said he needs at least a five percent as a down payment immediately and can't wait. It's going to be sold on a first come basis.

"If that was the only problem he had, hell I could give him a check right now for the down payment and we would close the deal later. So we both signed a contract of agreement and I told him my accountant will get in touch with him by the end of the week. Four days later my accountant did try to get in touch with this rascal but he never could find him. So I went over to the house to talk to him directly and when I drove up there I found different people living there. They told me they never heard of this Mr. Jones. They said they owned this property and had no intentions of selling it. I told the owner that I was just there a few days ago with Mr. Jones, and the place was not occupied. He said that it was impossible. They were out of town but they had the finest security system that money could buy, so I must have been at another address. There was no way that I could enter into their house without alerting his security people, he said. It was then that I realized that this bastard Jones swindled me out of one hundred thousand dollars.

"Like I said in the beginning, I don't know if this man is also your Bismarck Jones but after hearing all of these other swindles, I believe he fits the part."

"Thank you for your story, Mr. Gridley. I was just conferring with Mr. Wilson here about you and he tells me that yes, you were one of Mr. Jones's conquests. For some reason we didn't mail you a request to visit with us. I'm sorry for that, but your story confirms my suspicions that Bismarck Jones was into every conceivable swindle one can think of to extract money out of innocent people. The man is a down right criminal who has eluded the authorities for many years and I see no alternative today but to take matters into our own hands."

The Reverse Sting

Mr. Nichols stood up again to continued his discussion about Bismarck's life. "It seems that Bismarck is no longer in the Con business. He is now a legitimate business man worth millions. John tells me that he has changed a great deal. He is now beginning to enjoy himself, going to parties and nightclubs with a different young lady every night. He is now thirty years old and is considering settling down and raising a family but he hasn't found the right partner just yet. This is why I have invited Count Rocco's daughter, Lisa, here tonight."

There was suddenly a moment of stillness in the room but then they all began murmuring after Lisa's name was mentioned. Mr. Young from Australia then stood up and asked, "And how is she supposed to Con the great Bismarck?"

"That's all part of my plan. The first thing we must do is train Countess Lisa into becoming a professional gambler. She has to be very good at it or Bismarck will detect that she is a fraud and our efforts will be futile. She must gain his confidence and become his friend and possibly even his lover."

"Wait a minute, Mr. Nichols. I refuse to lower myself into becoming a prostitute with this man no matter what the cause. I already despise him for what he did to my father and now you want me to become his lover. Forget it."

"Now Countessa, hear me out. I don't expect you to go to bed with this man. I'm only asking you to entice him, make him fall in love with you. I have studied Bismarck's profile and his habits for the past few years and I'm sure you are the perfect woman to pull this thing off. He will be enthralled with you, believe me. He has a definite weakness for Italian ladies."

"And how am I supposed to become a professional gambler? I don't know anything about American card games."

"That's easy. Max Keller, alias Hans Miller, will teach you. You see Hans, I know who you are. Your refusal to tell us your story didn't disguise you in the least because I knew Mr. Keller personally. When you introduced yourself I knew you were a imposter right from the start. I immediately called my office and had you checked out and discovered that you are the brother of Karl Miller. You are here to avenge the death of your brother who was killed in a dual with Bismarck. I understand that you are a professional gambler yourself and maybe even better than your brother was. So you will be her tutor and you will train Countessa Lisa in the art of poker playing as well as blackjack. You will also act as her bodyguard in case things get out of hand. I also know that you were the amateur heavyweight boxing champion of Germany, so you should be able to handle the bodyguard assignment fairly easy."

Hans Miller didn't object. As a matter of fact he might even enjoy teaching this pretty lady the art of gambling and who knows what their relationship will be as they worked together. Lisa looked over Hans and didn't like the idea of being alone with this monster of a man, but she didn't protest either. She had to do something for her father's sake. What Mr. Nichols failed to omit telling her was that she would be hustling other men as part of her education and it could get pretty nasty if she was caught and challenged by the other card players. This is where Hans's strength will be utilized. Hopefully, it won't be necessary.

Nichols continued, "It's going to take some time to train her so don't expect miracles in a few weeks. Before she meets up with Bismarck she will first have to gamble with several real professionals. I'm giving you six months, Hans, to bring her up to the point where she can play competitively against Bismarck. This will also give everyone else in this room enough time to set him up for the kill with their own sting operations.

"You see, we cannot Con him in one big sweep. He's nobody's fool, and we couldn't Con him into making one single major investment. We must be smart and peck away at him with smaller investments. We will attack him from all angles slowly but surely, and after we break him of his millions we will all meet here again to celebrate. I'm confident my plan will work as long as everyone in this room does his or her job. We cannot have any slip ups. I will discuss with each and everyone of you your individual assignments and the role that you will play in this reverse sting operation.

"In order for our sting to work each one of you, except for Count Rocco and Miller, must be ready to contribute up to one million dollars to exercise your individual Con games or we can't win. It's going to be a ten million dollar reverse sting operation to conquer this man. If there's anyone in this room who does not want to participate, please say so now?"

"I don't think so, Mr. Nichols," said Mr. Schwartz. "Bismarck is very crafty and I don't think you can pull it off, so my wife and I have decided not to participate. We lost a lot of money by him but we are not poor. So we were taken by a crook. So what. Since we came to this country we have discovered that there are many ways one can be swindled. It was a learning experience for us and it taught us to be more careful the next time. Sometimes revenge can be more costly than you think. Anyway, we are leaving this evening and wish you all the luck in your reverse sting operation."

"Is there anyone else who wishes to leave?"

"I don't have a milliom to to contribute but I will participate," said Slick. There was no other response.

"Good. Now we will begin to work on your assignments. I'm going to discuss the assignments with each and every one of you separately so that no one knows what the other is doing. It will be safer that way. Hans and Lisa, you may leave right now and begin your project. Count Rocco, you may go back to Italy since we don't need you in this operation. I want to speak with Pietro first privately in my study because I know he has other very important engagements waiting for him. The rest of you may browse around the gardens, use the pool if you like, or go to your rooms but please do not leave the premises until you have received your assignment. Thank you."

The California Caper

Six months after Mr. Nichols concluded his meeting with his guests, Bismarck Jones flew to Southern California from New York for a vacation. Bismarck had accepted an invitation from a friend to use his beach house in Malibu, California, to relax and to just lounge around. The beach house was rather large and was located only a hundred yards from the ocean front. The view from the back porch overlooking the ocean was spectacular and on a clear day one could see Anacapa Island which is one of series of islands off the California coast known as The Channel Islands. Catalina Island and its famous city of Avalon is about forty miles to the south of Malibu and beyond the line of sight over the horizon. The porch of the house was coverted into a large screened in patio which opened into an uncovered deck that extended another ten feet. At the end of the deck were wooden rails that enclosed the outer edge of the patio except for a gated opening that lead to spiral stairs that descended to the sandy beach about twenty feet below.

Bismarck by this time was on the run from the mob and is now looking forward to a nice relaxing vacation away from the action. He was sure that no one but his friend knew that he left New York for Malibu. He didn't know that he was being spied upon by his personal valet who didn't travel with him but will be there in a day or so.

The next evening he was sitting on the back porch drinking a bourbon and water when he noticed a beautiful girl walking along the beach wearing a two-piece bathing suit. Her skin was tanned but her face was pure white as she protected it from the sun with a wide brim light blue colorful hat. Her hair was reddish brown which was laying softly down her back and on her shoulders. As she walked over the sand her hair would swing from side to side following her hip motion. Her bosom was exceptionally large in comparison with her tiny waste line. She had very shapely legs that Bismarck could not help but admire. She was rather tall and took slow long strides over the sand.

From Bismarck's view she was a dazzling and lovely sight to watch. As she strolled past him her shapely buttock moved from side to side in a well practiced manner. To Bismarck's eyes she was a captivating vision for him to behold. He was tempted to jump down there and try to meet her but he knew he was here to rest and to get away from it all. There were other girls in the area whom he could call upon if he so desired.

As she walked by him she glanced up and gave him a very sensual smile. He acknowledge her by waving his hand. She waved back but she didn't stop walking. She just kept smiling as she walked at the same pace while her red hair kept flipping from shoulder to shoulder. He continued to follow her with his eyes for a long while until she disappeared into another cottage further down the beach. The next evening there she was again. He couldn't resist himself this time and jumped over the porch railing and onto the sand. He then trotted over to her.

When she stopped to face him he said, "Excuse me, but I couldn't help admiring you from my porch."

She was, at first, startled over his dangerous vault down to the beach. "That was quite a leap. You could have hurt yourself." She sounded very concerned.

"It was nothing. I'm in top shape. Do you always take long walks on the beach this time of the day?"

"Yes I do. I like to stroll in the cool evenings when most of the bathers have gone home. It's so relaxing, don't you think? My name, by the way, is Lisa Drago and what may I ask is yours?"

Bismarck didn't expect it to be this easy, "Jones. William Jones. Do I detect an accent, Lisa?"

"Yes. I'm Italian by birth. I'm trying so hard to get rid of my accent but I guess I'm still not having that much success. `Jones?' That sounds like a British name. Were you born in England, Mr. Jones?"

"No. My ancestors, on my father's side, came over on the Mayflower, or so they tell me. They claim to be the original blue bloods of New England but I think they were forced to come to the colonies because of their criminal backgrounds and were moved to America to expand the population of New England in the New World. I'm pretty sure I've inherited some of their traits.

My mother was born in Germany, however.

"You are so modest, Mr. Jones. I'm sure you come from a fine upstanding family."

"Have it your way, but please call me Bill or William."

"Is that cottage your home, William?" She had a little trouble with the `W" and his name sounded more like Villiam.

"No. I'm just borrowing it from a friend. I have a home in Beverly Hills and I also have a home in up-state New York. I'm just out here from New York to get a little sunshine and relax at the beach. Would you care to step into my cottage for a refreshing drink?"

"Well, I suppose one cool drink might be nice, thank you, William."

Bismarck couldn't help admiring her body and was trying to avoid staring at her bosom. She was sure attractive and very charming. When they entered the cottage Bismarck began mixing her a martini. She said the only reason she preferred martinis was because she liked the taste of the saturated olive, and smiled. She had the most alluring smile that really enticed him.

"I'm actually just a simple girl, William. I was very lucky to be able come to this country. You see, an older lady friend of my mother's needed a companion to visit America with her, so I was very happy when I was asked to accompany her. As a matter of fact, in Europe I spent most of my time on the French Riviera working in the casinos as a card dealer. Do you like to gamble, William?"

Bismarck was starled by her gambling admission but simply answered, "Sometimes. I'm not really that good at cards. I go to Las Vegas now and again with a lady friend but I mostly watch her gamble at the slots. Once and a while I might try my luck at Black Jack."

"Well, if you ever want me to teach you some simple tricks to win at cards I will be glad to help you out, anytime."

"Thank you, Lisa. Maybe we can go to Vegas together sometime, that is, if your companion will allow you to leave her."

"Oh, my companion is no longer here. She left for Italy last month because she didn't feel very well, but I decided to remain. She said I could use her cottage free of charge as long as I want to. She's such a nice lady, but I really should start looking for work if I want to remain in America. Maybe Las Vegas could use a Black Jack dealer."

She began looking around the cottage and casually took a glimpse in the bedroom. Bismarck kept staring at her, following her every move. What a coincidence, he thought. It was almost too good to be true to find such an attractive Italian girl at a time when he was thinking of settling down and maybe getting married. His theory of European women was they made wonderful wives because European men dominate them the minute they are born. The man in Europe is master of his household and the women are still treated as second class citizens. Unlike American women who are always striving for equality and, in most cases, dominate the American male. At least that's the way he perceives married life in America. That was the way it was with his mother and father.

She then said to him, "Thank you for the drink, William, but I must be going. I have some friends coming over that will be playing poker and it is my job to act as hostess and deal the cards for them. My German friend, Hans Decker, insists that I deal all of the poker hands myself because he doesn't trust anyone else handling the cards. I make extra money doing this as I charge ten percent of each winning hand. But being a card dealer like this is only temporary because the men only get together every other week and sometimes longer. I do need a steady job."

"Is there anything serious between you and this friend, Hans?" asked Bismarck.

"Oh no... Of cause not. He's just a friend that I met in France. He's a gambler and that's the way he makes his living. Hans is really very good at it too. Maybe someday, you might want to join us, William."

"Yes. Maybe I will, someday."

She then went down the porch steps and back onto the beach, swaying her buttocks as she did before. Bismarck was getting disturbed again as he watched her walking away, but then he became very curious about her trade. He began thinking to himself about future gambling prospects. He had retired from the games when the Mafia began hunting him. He still misses the excitement of gambling by setting up a sting and enjoying the fun of finishing the game in triumph. What luck to find a beautiful girl who is also in the same business, he thought. He began thinking about all the future prospects and different ways he could use her in some new enterprises. If she's good, she could make an outstanding partner, especially if she was to become his wife. Together they could conquer the world. What a wonderful thought. But that's all it was, a thought or maybe just a romantic notion.

Meantime, the front door of the cottage began opening. It was John Wilson, Bismarck's valet, who was returning from an extended vacation.

"Good evening, John, and how was your vacation?"

"Excellent, Sir. I had the greatest time. I even met a gorgeous lady and I have to admit I'm getting serious over her. I'm even thinking of asking her to marry me. Her name is Cathy Sullivan from Ireland. Not only is she attractive but she's loaded."

Bismarck paused for a moment and thought it must be a coincident. Could it be his Cathy from Ireland? He was confused but simply remarked, "That's great. I guess then you will be leaving me soon?"

"No. Not for at least another six months, anyway. She now lives in New York and will be coming here to visit with me in a few weeks. That's when I'll pop the question. To be honest, I can't wait to see her again."

Something was not right. Why would Cathy consider a nobody such as John? His mind wasn't clear just yet. He was still thinking of Lisa. In any event, he knew that he will have to avoid ever meeting her again without a suitable disguise.

"That's wonderful, John. I'm happy for you. As a matter of fact, I think that I have also found a possible marital prospect myself. I just met her today, and I think she's the one, that is, if she'll have me. You know, I did mention to you that I was considering settling down and raising a family myself and it could just very well be this girl. Wait till you meet her, John.

She's absolutely stunning and she's Italian, not that it matters."

John kind of grinned to himself because he knew that Bismarck was particularly fond of European women especially Italian. He also knew that the set-up Mr. Nichols had in store for him was going along as planned. He then picked up his luggage and headed for his room.

The next day Lisa was again taken her evening stroll. Bismarck was anxiously waiting. He went down to greet her again but this time he asked her out to dinner. She smiled and accepted. Bismarck was now exceptionally happy. He knew she couldn't refuse him. He would even take bets on it. She headed back to her cottage to bathe and change for the evening. She wanted to be especially ravishing this evening to entice this knave and give him his just rewards. She hated to admit though that he was rather cute.

Bismarck picked her up in his Cadillac and took her to the Paradise Cove Restaurant which was famous for its sea food. Dinner dress was casual. He ordered Halibut for both of them and a bottle of their best wine. Their conversation was simple, talking about their pasts and their likes and dislikes. Bismarck, however, couldn't keep his eyes off of her. She was aware of his stares and every time she looked up she couldn't help but admire his fascinating blue eyes. After dinner they drove along route 1 known as the Pacific Coast Highway to an isolated area close to the beach. As they sat there together watching the motion of the ocean surf, Bismarck turned to admire her. She was some dish, he thought. He clumsily attempted to put his arm over her shoulder. At first she tried to stop him but then she gave in. She had to go along with the charade and eventually leaned toward him, resting her head on his shoulder. This game was knew to her and she didn't want to appear to be too anxious.

He said to her, "Lisa, you are absolutely beautiful. You're the most attractive girl that I have ever met. I don't know what it is about you but I feel so comfortable just being near you. I can't believe how lucky I am that I accidentally met you."

"I have to make a confession, William. You just didn't accidentally meet me. I planned it that way. You see, my next door neighbor told me there was an eligible bachelor living close by so I began taken my evening strolls hoping to meet you. Are you mad at me, William, for being so naughty?"

"Of course not. I'm glad you did."

He then leaned over and kissed her lips. She responded quite well and put her arms over his shoulder. He tried to put his hand on her breast but she slowly removed it. He just continued to kiss her and later made another attempt to touch her breast and again she rejected him.

She said, "Please William, we just met and I want to be sure about you. You see, I care for you a lot and I don't want you to have the wrong impression of me. I don't make it a habit of getting familiar with every man I meet, at least not on the first night. I made a promise to myself back home that I would save my feelings for the man that I truly love. I still don't know if you're that man, William. Please be patient with me."

"Ok, my sweet. I just want you to know that I'm infatuated with you and I think I'm falling in love with you."

"I'm having the same problem, William, but let's wait till we know each other a little better. How do I know that you haven't used that line on a dozen other girls before. You are a very handsome man and I'm sure you could get any girl you wanted."

"Well, I'll admit that I have had many dates with other women, but now that I've met you things will be different." He leaned over and kissed her again.

"I think you should take me home now, William, before I lose control of myself and who knows what will happen next. Please William."

"Very well. I do respect you for that but I warn you, I'll be coming after you every chance I can. I don't give up that easily." She just grinned.

He took her to her cottage but she didn't invite him in. She said that her German friend and some of the other players are in the middle of playing poker and she is sure they would want her to deal.

"When is your next poker party, Lisa? I may want to join you."

"This weekend. I'll save a spot for you but I must warn you these men play for high stakes. Are you sure you can handle it,

William?"

He said he was quite sure he could. Bismarck was not used to being rejected like this but then he figured she was only playing hard to get the first night out and he will eventually have her, especially after he cleans out the card table this weekend. When he returned to his own cottage his phone began ringing. It was Lisa.

"William, I hope you are not mad at me. I had such a wonderful time tonight. I just want you to know I do like you very much."

"Why should I be mad, my sweet? I told you I care for you very much myself but I have to admit I was a bit disappointed tonight. It's not that we are teenagers. We are mature adults and..."

"Forgive me, William. Maybe next time things will be a lot better. Good night my love," and she hung up leaving him a bit uncomfortable.

It was about eight o'clock Saturday evening when Bismarck showed up at Lisa's cottage. The day before he ordered two hundred thousand dollars in travelers checks from the Beverly Hills Bank Of America in ten thousand increments. He had the feeling that the stakes will be extra high and if the table stakes were the rules he didn't want to be caught short.

Seven-card stud was the game that night and when he arrived Lisa greeted him with a warm kiss at the door and escorted him to a chair at the card table. She introduced him to the other players as Mr. William Jones. They were all cordial and greeted him very friendly. What Bismarck didn't know was that they were all professional gamblers who were in cahoots together to destroy him. They were being well paid by Nichols to operate this scam. The object of this first attempt, as part of Mr. Nichols's overall plan, was to make him lose a substantial amount of money at each of these games so that he would eventually be forced out of retirement and go back into the Con racket again. Then the second phase of his plan would take effect which would involve Cathy Sullivan.

Lisa began dealing out the cards. Bismarck had already installed the sharp edge into his special altered finger as he had always done before the start of a card game. Hans wasn't completely sure how Bismarck marked the cards but he recently was able to obtain a deck of cards that Bismarck had previously played with. After he examining that deck under a microscope he noticed very thin scratches that appeared on the upper right hand corner which could not be seen with the naked eye. When he saw Bismarck put on his reading glasses he was now sure how he could read the cards. He was impressed. He suspected that they were being marked but he wasn't sure how.

Each of the players had been assigned a different playing method to foul up Bismarck's marked cards. Hans also had a sharp object in his vest pocket which he would use to add to Bismarck's scratches thus making him read the cards incorrectly. Hans had to be careful and not use this technique too often or Bismarck might get wise. This is why the other players were there, to confuse him using different methods of distorting Bismarck's marked cards or by distracting him. One player used the switching card approach. By replacing a three, for example, with an ace, which he took out from under his sleeve, Bismarck's game plan would be disrupted because there would be extra aces in the deck. But they would only do this when the stakes were very high. They knew that it would take a few hands for Bismarck to mark enough cards before he would be ready to get into the big money. Even Lisa played an important roll during this caper. She would periodically switch decks after a few rounds so that the cards that Bismarck marked would be gone. He also caught her dealing from the bottom.

The games began and Bismarck patiently began marking the cards as he had always done many times before. He was losing small bets in the beginning as usual. When the pot was up to ten thousand dollars he bet heavily and sure enough they would let him win. When he detected Lisa switching cards again he had to go back to marking them again. This time the pot was up to fifty thousand dollars and he began noticing that the scratches he made were clumsily altered. He figured that someone was wise to his racket but he didn't panic. In this case he simply ignored the second scratches because they were crudely done. He still knew where the aces and pitcher cards were. He was not supposed to win the fifty grand pot, but he did.

Bismarck didn't have to watch Lisa switching cards any longer. When his marks disappeared he knew they were switched. He was kind of mad at the set-up and especially with Lisa for being a party to this scam.

The next pot went all the way up to a hundred thousand dollars. Bismarck knew that this was the final set-up to break him. He had to resort to another tactic, so he went back to his own card switching routine but in reverse. On several previous hands he noticed an ace was inserted that was unmarked so he would replace it with a duce. Pretty soon the deck was loaded with duces. He was now ready for the kill. He raise the bet by one hundred thousand dollars. All but Hans and another player dropped out of the game. He matched Bismarck's bet and raised him another hundred grand. Bismarck was now at his table stake limit. He couldn't raise no longer. He finally called the bet. Hans showed his hand and produced four duces. The other player also had four duces but he couldn't disclose his hand or Bismarck would know they were cheating. Bismarck immediately placed his hand on the table showing four aces. He won five hundred thousand dollars in that one game. Hans couldn't stand the defeat and immediately stood up, flipped the card table over and produced a pistol.

"You cheating bastard," he yelled. But before he fired Bismarck quickly drew his own gun from under his coat and shot and killed Hans right on the spot. The noise was deafening. Lisa screamed when another player produced a gun. Bismarck turned swiftly and shot this other man dead.

"Anyone else want to try their luck?" he yelled.

Suddenly the room became quiet. No one moved. Even Lisa was stunned and remained motionless. Bismarck simply cashed in his chips, put all of the money in his coat pocket and walked out the door.

The police arrived later that evening and after questioning everyone the sergeant in charge walked over to Bismarck's cottage.

"You claim it was self defense, Mr. Jones?"

"Yes, Sergeant. I won a sizable amount of money playing

poker fair and square but this Hans guy couldn't handle the loss. He fell apart and accused me of cheating him and tried to kill me. I had no choice but to defend myself and shoot him first."

"Do you have a permit for your gun, Mr. Jones."

"Yes I do, Sergeant."

"Well, in any case, I'm taken you into headquarters for illegal gambling."

Bismarck gave no resistance and went along with him quietly. He was later fined one thousand dollars by a local judge for illegal gambling and was set free. It also had cost him twenty grand to buy off the judge but that's the price one has to pay to stay in this rotten business.

Lisa was waiting for him outside the county jail after he was released.

"What do you want?" asked Bismarck very harshly.

"Please William. I need to talk to you."

He looked at her curiously but then he finally agreed. He had to admit she was still some looker so they went to his cottage again. John Wilson eyed her very carefully as she entered the cabin. He didn't know if she had become a turn-coat or was still following Mr. Nichols's plan.

"John," Bismarck said after a short introduction, "Would you please excuse us."

John said he had to do some shopping at the local grocery store and would be back in a couple of hours.

After he left Bismarck began his interrogation, "Now, my dear Lisa, what phoney tale do you wish to discuss with me this time?"

"Please, William. I know what you must think of me. I had no choice. I will admit that I was a party to that sting but that was before I met the real you. Hans set up the whole thing. You see, his real name is not Decker. It's Miller. He claims that you killed his brother in a dual at Monte Carlo and he wanted to get his revenge. When he met me in the casino in France he offered me this job to entice you into playing cards. He wanted to break you of all of your money and make you a pauper. He said he would eventually kill you and avenge his brother's death but he wanted you to suffer first. Like I said, William, that was before I met you and I didn't expect to fall in love with you. I wanted to bow out of that game that evening but then he had threatened me. I had no choice but to do my part. I must admit I was thrilled when I saw you lay down those four aces. It was stroke of genius the way you handled those cards. They say you are the greatest card player in the world and now I believe it's true. Please forgive me, my love. I'm just a victim of circumstances. I'm really just an innocent bystander who was trying to make some extra money." She began sobbing.

"I must say, Lisa, this is some line of bull you just gave me. I don't believe a word of it."

"But you must, William. I now have nowhere to go. I'm all alone in this country. What am I to do? I don't even have enough money to go back to Italy. Please, William. Won't you give me another chance? You'll see. I'll make it up to you, I promise you."

"In that case, prove it. Prove it to me this very night in my bed."

Lisa didn't expect that. She was sure she could convince him that she was still in love with him but now she was faced with a different ultimatum. The real reason she went this far was because Mr. Nichols had convinced her to continue her effort. He knew of Bismarck's weakness and was sure she could get back into his good graces.

She finally agreed to make love with him. She couldn't see her way out. Besides, she sort of liked him and was very impressed with the way he handled Hans and the other men. She was a bit fascinated with the thrill of intrigue and danger herself. It was in her Italian blood. His actions gave her a different perspective of this great Con artist. Her hatred of him was slowly changing to admiration.

"William, I must warn you. This will be only the second time I went to bed with a man so I'm not too good at it. You will be patient with me, please, and show me the way?"

"Who was the first man, if I may ask?"

"I'd rather not talk about him, not just yet. It was such a horrible experience for me and since then I have refused to have an affair with any other man. This is why I am still single at twenty eight which is unheard of in Europe. I will tell you the story someday, when we become more intimate. Please be gentle with me, William. I want this to be a pleasant experience. I couldn't stand another bad relationship."

Bismarck was still a little bitter. He didn't know whether to buy her act or turn her out. He figured at least he will have her and he will know in bed if she is faking it. He had loved many women throughout his life and knows all the symptoms of a bad actress.

He began to calm down. He was so elated at the prospect of making love with this beauty that he finally let his guard down and began kissing her passionately. He again tried to place his hand on her breast and this time she didn't stop him. He unfastened her bra from the front which invariably exposed her beautiful creamy breasts that glowed white over her contrasting tanned shoulders. He lowered his lips to her nipples and began sucking them one at a time. He then began to remove her dress and for a just moment he stood over her to observed her striking body with her long legs dangling over the edge of the bed. He couldn't wait any longer. He had to have her so he quickly removed his own clothing and mounted her.

When they initially began their intercourse it was just to prove something. He thought he would use her just to satisfy his manly necessities and she thought she would simply give in to him to do Mr. Nichols's bidding, but the affair was slowly changing from just a plain intercourse for sex to a romance that neither one could understand. Their love making was no longer an encounter of two rivals but was now a serious and sensual reality. They both reached their sexual peaks together and their mutual explosion was the conclusive evidence of a bond that may never be broken. When she reach her own climax she began screaming as though she was in pain but then she hugged him tightly. This was a new experience for her. They kissed each other as though they had just discovered a lost love for the first time.

Bismarck was the first to stand up and walk around the room confused and finally sat in a chair near by. Lisa just watched him not saying a word. It was an awkward moment for both of them.

Lisa knew that she was actually falling in love with him even though she had promised herself that she would destroy him for what he had done to her father. She couldn't understand this new infatuation. How could she deceive her father by falling in love with his enemy? Her mind was so mixed up.

He was also unsure of himself of what was going on in his brain. He knew, for some unexplained reason, he wanted her forever, even after what she had done to him. After a moment of contemplating his future he finally came to a decision. She will be his forever. He went back to the bed and kissed her and made passionate love with her again. It was no longer a contest between them, for they were now truly in love with each other.

Later that evening, they began talking once again and their conversation continued late into the night. They made love several more times with equal fulfillment and finally the next morning she left him. She went back to Italy that same day to be with her father. Lisa didn't even inform Mr. Nichols of her departure. When Mr. Nichols finally was informed of her exodus and of the death of Miller he was furious.

Cathy Sullivan's Con Attempt

Cathy Sullivan was flying out to California to visit her new boyfriend, John Wilson. Bismarck told John that he would have to greet her with a different disguise, as a Mr. Thompson because he was still working on a special Con job and didn't want to have to go back and forth with different faces. He promised that he would meet her eventually with his own face. John knew about their previous relationship in Ireland when he jilted her as Mr. John Smith. He just went along with the charade. Mr. Nichols also knew that Bismarck couldn't resist stealing from the same mark twice so his plan was to set him up into thinking that this time he could Con money out of Cathy instead of her aunt. The last time he swindled her aunt out of two hundred thousand pounds. Cathy was even wealthier than her aunt and would make a lucrative mark. The bait was set.

The day she arrived at Bismarck's cottage John introduced him to Cathy as Mr. Thompson who is considered to be a great Hollywood producer. Bismarck's disguise was perfect. He looked as though he was in his late sixties with a full beard and grey hair. As he approached her he walked slowly with a cane and was stooped over a bit. There was no resemblance between Mr. Thompson and Mr. William Jones. The disguise that he used when he was courting her aunt back in Ireland was completely different.

She was not told by Mr. Nichols or by Wilson that Mr. Thompson was Mr. William Jones or Bismarck Jones, alias John Smith. Mr. Nichols was planning to catch him in the act of Conning her and then notify the authorities. By her not knowing who he was she wouldn't have to act the part. This way it would be a natural assignment. Nichols knew that Bismarck would some how try to Con her. He couldn't help himself when it comes to an easy prey. The only problem that remains in Bismarck's mind is Miss Sullivan's beauty. He still recalls the love affair they had together in Ireland but he must control himself, especially now that he met Lisa.

"Good evening, Miss Sullivan. John has spoken so much about you. I can see he wasn't exaggerating. You are very pretty."

"Thank you, Mr. Thompson. You're very kind." Her Irish brogue was still prevalent.

After the introductions John made an excuse that he had to go back to the airport because Miss Sullivan had claimed that she was still missing one luggage piece. While he was gone it was a good opportunity for Bismarck to swing into action.

"Have you ever done any serious acting before, Miss Sullivan?"

"Well, yes. I did do a stage play as a maid in Dublin a year ago but nothing too spectacular, I'm afraid."

"I understand that John has mentioned to you that I am a Hollywood producer in the process of making a new movie. I've been auditioning several young women for my leading lady and after meeting you I believe I have just discovered her. My new movie, IT'S A SHINING LIGHT is being delayed until I select a star. Would you consider having a screen test for me, my dear."

"My goodness. Are you serious, Mr. Thompson?"

"I definitely think you would be perfect for the part."

"I can't believe this is happening to me. I would be delighted to have a screen test. Thank you so much, Mr. Thompson." She was indeed happy at the prospect.

"Now I don't want you to say one word about this to anyone not even to John. It will be just our little secret, okay? Then, if you are accepted, we will announce it to the world."

"Oh, Mr. Thompson. I'm so thrilled." She was excited.

John had casually mentioned to Bismarck that Cathy was interested in investing a large sum in the movies industry in California and this is what gave Bismarck the idea of Conning her into becoming a movie actress, with him as the producer.

"John tells me that you are considering making an investment into the movie business. Well, it just so happens that my company, ABM, is considering selling some shares in the corporation. But it all depends on this movie I am now producing. I am willing to invest one million dollars of my own money if I could find an equal investor... You know, a thought just occurred to me. You could own your own movie and also be the star. It would be a perfect set up, don't you agree?"

She said, "I don't know what to say, Mr. Thompson. Do you really think I could be a STAR and own my own movie?"

Bismarck knew he was convincing enough and said to her that she would be the most sensational actress in the country inside of two years, but he also needed her investment as soon as possible to start off her career properly.

Cathy said she would agree after she talked with her accountant. She made a phone call and after a long discussion she finally agreed. However, she stipulated that the finances must be handled by her accountant, Jason, who is here in California. She also said that her money was tied up in Ireland but she did have her jewelry with her that was worth considerably more than a million dollars and it could be used as collateral to borrow the million as needed from a local bank.

Bismarck was not happy with this arrangement but he finally agreed. He figured he has never met an accountant he couldn't swindle, so he accepted the terms. He didn't know, however, that she was actually talking to Mr. Nichols on the phone instead and that Jason was not really an accountant but a Private Eye who would combine their total investment and disappear with it. Cathy then, would get her jewelry back later. It was a perfect set-up, Nichols thought.

When Bismarck's valet came back, he made a pathetic excuse that he will have to go back to New York to visit his sick mother and would he take care of Cathy while he was away. Bismarck agreed and was elated now because he could operate this scam freely. Actually, John was now having a mental problem with his relationship with both Mr. Nichols and Bismarck. Mr. Nichols paid him well but Bismarck paid him considerably more. At first he relished the idea of pulling a double sting on Bismarck, but after working for him now for seven years he wasn't too sure he wanted to go through with the reverse sting any longer. He was having seconds thoughts about the whole set-up.

He said to himself, "What will happen to me when it's all

over? I'll be out of a job and Bismarck will be broke or possibly be dead. If he lives he may even try to kill me for my role in this reverse sting operation." He was becoming despondent over the whole affair.

He really liked working as Bismarck's valet and thought to himself that if Bismarck won out over this sting, he would remain as his valet and continue working for him. He never wanted to get married himself in the first place as long as he could have a girlfriend or two in town. The thought of raising a family never entered his mind. Then again, when he thought about the Mafia being involved in this caper, he decided he wanted no part of this reverse sting any longer, so he trumped up this excuse that he had to leave town, but fast. Things will be happening pretty quick around here especially if this latest bust doesn't work out, he thought.

The fake screen test was set up for Cathy and, of course, she passed with flying colors. Bismarck hired a full crew who had worked for him before on different scams and were professional extortionists themselves. These men were so skilled in the movie business they would have no trouble convincing anyone that they were a legitimate movie studio. They were certainly first class pros.

Bismarck needed the time to make sure her jewelry was safe in the hands of her so called accountant, Jason, before he turned over his own one million dollars. The accountant for the moment had Cathy's jewelry, worth two million dollars, locked in his safe at his home in Santa Barbara, California, about two hours north of Malabu. Tomorrow, he said he will obtain the loan for Cathy and transfer all of her assets to a bank in Southern California to finance the movie. Bismarck had to work fast. While Jason was still in Los Angeles negotiating with the Bank of America, Bismarck drove north to the city of Santa Barbara.

Jason's home was well guarded with German Shepherds that roamed the estate freely. Jason also has the latest security alarm system installed. It won't be easy to break in. Bismarck waited till that evening in town to obtain a few things and then went to the back of the estate. He hid himself under a large oak tree till dark. He then heaved several rib steaks over the wall for the guard dogs to feed on. He could hear the animals on the other side of the wall gouging themselves on tranquilized steaks. Bismarck didn't mind killing in self defense but he did have a soft spot for animals so he didn't use poison. After the dogs were asleep he scaled the wall. He was dressed in a completely black outfit with his face covered with charcoal. The task now was to disable the alarm system.

Before Bismarck went to Santa Barbara he paid a visit with an old friend that was an expert in security systems. For ten thousand dollars his friend gave him an accelerated course in the operation on Jason's security system. If there was a way to disable it, Bismarck's friend knew how.

Bismarck had to climb up a wall located in the back of the building. He made his way up to the roof and finally located the main control electronics of the security system by following a large bundle of wires laying across the roof that ended up inside an attic room. When he looked over the edge of the roof he noticed that there was no easy access to the window of this attic room but, fortunately, there was no security sensor installed there. Bismarck then lower himself down from the roof to the attic window with a rope anchored around a chimminy and because the window was recessed he had to reach out with his foot to smash the window. He then swayed himself on the rope back and forth until he was able to reach the attic window to grab the sill. He then was able to climb in the window and after a short period he disabled the security system. When he went down stairs he began looking in each room for a safe. Bismarck finally found the safe hidden behind an abstract painting in the study. The safe was no problem for him. He became an expert in safe cracking over the many years on different capers. He initially learned about safe cracking through another friend who is now in the pen serving time. Bismarck knew he could always buy such information as long as he paid the right price in cash.

A few days later Cathy headed for the studio to continue the movie. They were getting ready to shoot a very important love scene and she was so involved with the movie by now that she couldn't wait to get there. She drove to the front gate as usual but for no apparent there was no guard at the entrance. The front gate was wide open so she drove directly to the studio building. Again, no one was around. She entered the studio and the place seemed deserted. Cathy then drove back to Bismarck's cottage at the beach and it was also empty. The phone rang. She reluctantly picked up the receiver. It was Jason. He was hysterical. He finally calmed down and said his home had been burglarized and her jewelry, worth two-million dollars, was stolen. She fainted. Bismarck sold the jewelry to a fence for one third their worth. He was satisfied with the money but was especially thrilled with the whole operation. Winning a Con game was always his greatest passion. The money was just a secondary reward. He would have loved to see Nichols's face when he found out about this latest failure.

Bismarck was having a ball.

Slick Barny's Revenge

Bismarck's disappearance and this latest sting operation that backfired made Mr. Nichols even more furious. Two reverse sting attempts so far have failed and that bastard Bismarck is still running loose, he thought. He couldn't even locate John Wilson. He finally had to enlist Pietro Columbo's soldiers to help find John. The search went on for a year and John was finally located by a member of the Chicago mob. He was picked up and taken directly to Mr. Nichols.

"Where have you been?" asked Mr. Nichols.

John nervously said, "After what happened on those last two capers I was afraid Bismarck was getting wise to me so I skipped town."

"Bull shit. You were supposed to stay with Cathy to make sure things ran smoothly and you were supposed to inform me on any movement that Bismarck made. The sun-of-a-bitch stole Cathy's jewelry worth two million dollars."

"I'm sorry, boss. It couldn't be helped. I was afraid for my life." Actually, John was pleased to learn that Bismarck had gotten away with that caper.

"Where is he now?" asked Mr. Nichols.

"I don't know, believe me." In a way he was trying to protect Bismarck. He didn't anticipate Nichols next move.

"Make him talk." He said to one of Pietro's goons.

The man he addressed was built like a line backer with huge forearms. He first began beating Wilson in the stomach and then in the face. Wilson wasn't a strong man and knew sooner or later he would have to give in.

"Alright, alright. I'll tell you," as he held his stomach with both hands. "He's some place in Long Island, New York. He sometimes goes there to hide out after a successful sting to allow things to cool off."

"Good. That will make a nice set-up for our next project which will be conducted by Mr. James Barnum, alias Slick Barny," said Mr. Nichols while drinking a glass of wine. "You better be telling the truth or the mob will hunt you down again and this time it will for keeps. Meanwhile you're fired so get the hell out of my sight."

Nichols began grinning to himself at the prospect of what Slick might do to that crook. Slick will find him and if he kills Bismarck that will end the project, he thought. If he misses then the Mafia will surely finish him off. Nichols was no longer interested in getting the money back for the victims or breaking Bismarck financially. He now wanted complete revenge at any cost.

Without mentioning it to Nichols, John Wilson went to Babylon where he knew Bismarck would be in hiding. He was hoping he could get back into Bismarck's good graces. He took the Long Island railroad from Manhattan and rented a car at the station in Valley Stream. Unfortunately, he didn't know that he was being followed. He drove to Bismarck's resident which was located near Sunrise High Way in Babylon and parked across the street from Bismarck's home. At this point he was very cautious. He didn't want to just barge in or even knock on the door because he knew Bismarck was in hiding and may shoot first through the door. He just sat there hoping Bismarck might recognize him on his way home. Sure enough an hour later his car door opened and a gun was thrust into his face.

The gun man asked, "Are you alone?"

John responded, "Yes. Please don't shoot."

The gun was slowly removed. When John turned and saw it was Bismarck, he was relieved. He thought it was one of the mob.

Bismarck said, "Come into the house. You have a lot of explaining to do."

They both walked across the street and entered a small two bedroom home not at all like his mansion in up-state New York. John was told to sit down and start explaining what had happened to him.

He began by saying, "I didn't know what to do boss. When I got back from visiting my mother the cottage in Malibu was crawling with cops. I figure I'd better not get involved so I took off. I drove the Cadillac to Washington State and later to

Colorado. I didn't want to stay in one place too long so I kept on moving. After awhile my money ran out and I thought maybe you may have come here to hide out. I gave it a try and here I am."

"So you weren't questioned by the police?"

"No sir. They never got to me," answered his valet. He never mentioned Nichols.

"Okay. We will stay low here for awhile until I'm sure the coast is clear, and then we'll head for England. Fortunately, I have a substantial account in England as well as other places so I won't have to approach a U.S. bank just yet. Somebody is after me, John. I don't know who it is. Those last two incidents at the Malibu were no accident. I knew that card game was fixed but I'm still puzzled about how Cathy Sullivan fits in. How did you meet her?

"Actually she met me. Now that you mention it, I'm willing to bet that someone was using me to get to you through Cathy. It was rather strange the way she came on to me. As you can see, I'm really not that attractive and when she approached me in the lobby at the Biltmore Hotel I couldn't believe such a beautiful girl would even talk to me. At first I thought she might be a hooker but after I examined the register I knew she was for real. I can see now she was really after you through me for what you did to her aunt in Ireland. I never saw her in Ireland and I didn't connect the name. I'm sorry chief. It looks like I messed things up for you."

"Oh, that's all right, John. I think there's a master plan behind all of these coincidences. First of all, there was Lisa setting me up for Hans Miller and now Cathy. They're all after me for revenge or to get their money back. I wonder who will be next to attempt to sting me?"

John Wilson was relieved. Bismarck bought his story so he went back to being a valet again, tidying up and preparing dinner. He really liked this job and was glad that Bismarck came out of those encounters without a scratch. He thought about telling him about Slick Barny but then he would have to reveal himself about working for Mr. Nichols. What a crazy predicament he got himself into.

The next few days Bismarck began frequenting the local pool hall. He was getting restless laying around in that small home and missed the gambling action so he would go to the pool hall and play a few friendly games but avoided any serious large bets. After awhile he became very friendly with the local men and one in particular, Carlo Franco. Carlo was a short man of Italian extraction who was in his thirties. Bismarck observed that he was an excellent pool player but he was sure he could take him if the chips were down. Franco was a hustler himself and tried several times to get Bismarck into a betting game.

Bismarck's response was, "No thank you. Your too good for me, Carlo. It would be like you taking candy from a baby. You better find another patsy."

They would play for fun against one another and Bismarck would intentionally miss sinking a ball and let Carlo win. Bismarck just liked the atmosphere and the clowning around that usually goes on in such places. Then one day a stranger came in and put his fifty-cent piece on the table to challenge the winner between Bismarck and Carlo. Carlo looked up at this stranger and began licking his chops. He then finished the run against Bismarck and asked the guy what kind of a game did he want to play.

The stranger said, "Eight ball. One hundred bucks a game."

Carlo quickly remarked, "Your on, pal."

Bismarck watched the game from the bar. Fortunately, Bismarck recognized the man as one of Slick Barny's goons. This immediately alerted him that there might be another attempt to extract money from him or even worse, to kill him. He reached behind his back to make sure his gun was still in place. He was now ready for whatever outcome followed.

Game after game the stranger was beating Carlo. At first Bismarck thought that Carlo was merely trying to set him up for the big kill but then Carlo came over and whispered to him.

"Listen, Bill. This guy is too good for me. I already lost a thousand bucks. I can't afford any more."

Bismarck could see his friend was getting desperate so he casually put his own fifty-cent piece on the table and said out loud, "A thousand bucks, man."

Carlo was astonished. He thought Bismarck was crazy. He just told him that this man is too good for himself and now he wants to challenge him. He had no trouble in beating Bill many times. He tried once more to stop him but Bismarck simply pushed his arm away. Carlo simply raised his arms in discussed.

The stranger accepted the challenge and the game was on. Bismarck toyed with him at first but then he easily won four racks in a row and pocketed the money. The frustrated stranger excused himself and went outside. When he returned he was with a friend who remained back in the shadows at the other end of the bar. The same stranger walked over to Bismarck and offered to ante up the bet to ten thousand dollars but this time in straight pool. This maneuver puzzled Bismarck but he agreed and again he won with no difficulty. The stranger said double or nothing and Bismarck won again.

The stranger's friend finally came from behind the bar and Bismarck immediately recognized him as Slick Barny. His early assumption was correct. Slick took over the stick from his friend and said one hundred thousand. Bismarck said he didn't have that much on him. Slick said he would accept his marker. Bismarck now knew that money was not the stakes here. He had no choice so he accepted the challenge. They flipped a coin to see who will go first and Slick won. The contest was on. Slick ran the first table and on the break in the second rack he lost his turn. Bismarck ran the next four tables and won the game. Slick reached into his canvas back and pulled out one hundred-grand in thousand dollar bills and handed it to Bismarck. He then left the pool hall with the stranger. Carlo, who was standing near by, was flabbergasted. He had never see so much money in his life. Bismarck then separated ten thousand from the stack and gave it to Carlo who was absolutely dumbfounded. Bismarck then put on his coat and was ready to meet whatever fate faced him out the front door. He knew Slick and his buddy would be waiting for him.

Bismarck was usually prepared for such events but this time he couldn't see any escape route. He quickly made a phone call to John hoping that he may come up with something. He wasn't sure he wanted to accept this confrontation so before he stepped out he walked over to the bar and asked the bartender if there was a back exit. He was told that he could go out the bathroom window. Bismarck then walked through the bar and quickly entered the bathroom. He shut the light so as not to be seen escaping through the window. He slowly opened the window and waited. He finally made his move. As he began to climb out he heard gun shots. He thought the shots were meant for him but then he saw a man, who was hiding behind a dark entrance, fall to the ground. The man was obviously waiting for him. Bismarck didn't know for sure who was doing the shooting and wasn't waiting to find out.

He jumped out of the window and began running as fast as he could. All of a sudden there was a steady blast of gun fire behind him but nothing was coming his way. He stopped to look back and saw Slick Barny falling to the ground at the pool hall entrance from gunshot. As Bismarck ran passed the first man that was shot down he saw it was the stranger who played pool against him. He was obviously dead. Then another man came running toward him. Bismarck was about to open fire on this man but then he recognized who gun-man was. It was John, his valet. Bismarck was relieved. Together they headed for his Cadillac that was parked close by and on the way they passed Slick's body. Bismarck couldn't help himself and reached down and grabbed Slick's canvas bag containing thousands of dollars. With John at the wheel, they drove away at a good clip but they didn't go back to the house. Instead they took the Belt Parkway and drove out of town through Queens and Brooklyn and directly to Manhattan toward the New York waterfront on the Hudson river. Bismarck later booked passages on the Mauretania that happened to be heading for England. Slick's canvas bag had an additional one-hundred thousand dollars in it so Bismarck handed the bag over to John.

He simply said to John, "Thanks partner. You've earned every bit of it."

From then on Bismarck made John an equal partner in any new enterprise. John accepted, but he still wanted to continue to be his valet. They shook hands over their newly found relationship.

In England

Bismarck and John Wilson arrived in England on January 5, 1935. Bismarck was now 31 years old. He immediately purchased a home on the outskirts of London and for the most part they kept to themselves. Bismarck began using an alias and now calls himself William Perkins.

John continued acting as Bismarcks valet but decided to hire a maid and male cook. Since he was now a full partner he didn't particularly care to do the menial chores any longer so he began looking for help. Before John hired the help he had interviewed at least one-hundred prospects for both jobs. His requirements for the maid was a bit unusual. She had to be rather young, in her twenties or early thirties and had to be attractive but not necessarily beautiful. John's final choice for the maid was a Miss Mary Stewart whose only prerequisite was that she came from a broken home but seemed be exceptionally charming. Even though she had limited experiences as a maid John seemed to be attracted to her. Mary's hair was blond which laid straight down on her shoulders and covered the sides of her rather attractive face. She was a little short, about five foot-one inches and slightly overweight but John preferred his women that way. Most of his lady friends were always pleasantly plump.

The main reason she was selected was that both Mary's father and mother were serving time for extortion and she was honest enough to divulge this information. Besides being very cooperative and cheerful she had also dabbled in gambling. John was afraid to hire a normal professional maid because of Bismarck's devious background. It turned out that she also had served some time in jail as a shop lifter and was just recently released from prison. A law abiding maid might be inclined to inform Scotland Yard if she overheard any criminalistic conversations between him and Bismarck. John needed someone he could trust and Mary fit that bill.

The cook he selected was a Frenchman, Pierre La Roach,

who had excellent credentials in gourmet cooking. The only problem was that he seemed to be gay. Regardless, his sexual preference was fine with John because this would assure him that there would be no hanky panky going on between the cook and the maid. Also, the fact that his English was poor and the chances of him picking up incriminating conversations would be minimal. It turned out to be a perfect arrangement. Mary took care of the house and Pierre took care of the kitchen.

When Bismarck went to London for his own entertainment, John began taking more notice of Mary as she worked around the house. He began helping her move furniture when needed and started hanging around the kitchen often with her at tea time. Mary was well aware of his intentions and she didn't discourage him. She's been around and knew that she was attractive to most older men. Her last maid's job lasted only three months because she was caught in bed with the owner by his wife. Going to bed with John wouldn't cause her to lose her job, she thought, since he is single. She waited for him to make the first move, however. She even began teasing him a bit and encouraging his advances by bending over at the right moment to dust so that he could see her underwear.

John finally got up the courage and ask her if she would care to go for a drive in the country. She promptly agreed. They took Bismarck's Jaguar convertible and with the top down they drove around the open country. He began driving faster and faster. She didn't mind the speed at all and was laughing every time he made a quick turn. He eventually stopped at a stream and they sat there for awhile looking at the flow of the water not saying a word to each other. He finally couldn't wait any longer and put his arm around her and pulled her towards him and began kissing her rather roughly.

He quickly released her and apologized, "I'm sorry, Mary. I just couldn't help myself. I think I'm falling in love with you."

"What are we going to do, John. Will Mr. Perkins disapprove of us for being in love."

"You mean, you also love me?"

"Yes I do, John."

He immediately hugged her again very tightly and kissed her

over and over again. After a bit he said, "I don't care if Mr. Perkins approves of our relationship or not. I want you, Mary, and no one is going to stop that. You see, I have never been in love before so it didn't bother me being Mr. Perkins valet. But now I have to think of our future, and if he fires you I will also leave him. I have some money stashed away and we could do quite well."

"Please John. Think about it some more. Don't make any rash decisions."

"Mary, there's nothing to decide. I love you and you love me. The decision has already been made."

They drove to a hotel and in no time they were in bed together. After that situation their love affair continued for several months. At first they were discrete and used the same hotel which was located about twenty kilometers from Bismarck's home. After awhile she became more bold and would sneak up to his bedroom and spend the night in his bed. Bismarck was becoming aware of their activities so one day he asked John to join him for a brandy after dinner.

"John. I'm going to be frank with you. I'm not blind you know. I could tell that you and Mary have something going on between you. Would you care to discuss it with me?"

"Yeah, sure boss. It's true. I tried to keep it from you because I was afraid you would fire her and I was afraid of losing her. We love each other very much."

"Very well then. There is only one way that she can remain here and that is if you were married. I can't have a girl living here who might be used by the authorities to incriminate me. As husband and wife she wouldn't be so eager to testify against her husband or to disclose our activities. What's it going to be, John, marriage or dismissal?"

John immediately responded, "Marriage."

It turned out to be a small wedding since neither the bride nor the groom had many friends or relatives in England. Mary's parents were still in jail and she only had one sister whom she hasn't seen in ten years. They were married in the chapel of a Presbyterian church and, for a wedding present, Bismarck gave them an all expense paid honeymoon in Italy. John and Mary were married in June of 1935.

When they returned from their honeymoon John began relating all of his experiences he had found in Italy. He told Bismarck, "The Fascists are killing thousands of people and Italy's army is building up rapidly, preparing for the invasion of Abyssinia. Mussolini is on a rampage. He makes such statements as: `War is to man what maternity is to woman.' It looks to me that we may be in for another world war, Bill."

Bismarck had previously asked John, "If you get a chance in Milan see if you could locate Countessa Lisa Marabito for me." On that score John reported that her Father Count Rocco had died and that the Countessa was now married to a Fascist general. Bismarck was a bit disappointed about this unfortunate news but then what did he expect. After all, he hadn't corresponded with her since she had left America and returned to Italy. He still had feelings for her, but now it seems hopeless. He let a good one get away, he thought.

In that last night at the cottage in Malibu, California, Lisa had confessed everything to Bismarck. He was made aware of John's association with Mr. Nichols as a spy tracking his every move. Bismarck decided then that he would have to, eventually, eliminate John. As it turned out, however, John saved his life and then became his most trusted friend. Bismarck never told John that he knew all about his arrangement with Mr. Nichols. What was the point? Bismarck also promised Lisa that as soon as he cleared up a few thing in America he would join her in Italy, but because he was on the run from the mob he never contacted her for fear of her life. He knew the Mafia connection in Italy would question her to get to him. They might even eliminate her if they were so inclined. Bismarck couldn't take that chance.

Over the next few years their lives in England were rather simple except John and Mary had a child and they named it William after Bismarck. The boy would call Bismarck Uncle Bill as he grew older. Bismarck was proud of that boy and played with him often, teaching him card tricks when he was older. He didn't indulge in any more Con games and purposely stayed away from all gambling activities.

Bismarck's love life also followed a simple pattern. He never brought a lady companion home with him. His love affairs were discrete and were carried on away from his London home. He generally went either to Scotland or Ireland for long periods of time with a woman. He even resumed a second love affair with Cathy Sullivan in Ireland. By now she knew who he was and still accepted him. She loved him so much she didn't care about his past. The affair was getting serious and Cathy's mother was again becoming furious with her and told her that she should either marry him or dump him.

One evening, in the same Hotel where they had their first sexual affair, she said to him, "William, we've been going together now for two years. I have to know what your plans are for our future. I can't stand it this way"

He sat up in the bed and said, "Cathy, I must confess to you. I enjoy being with you and I do love you very much but marriage is out of the question at this time. With my reputation and the way I make a living it would be unfair to you or to our family. The way it is now I could be killed by my enemies or arrested by the authorities at any moment. My life is hanging on a very thin thread. Even now I'm in hiding because a New York Mafia chief is after me. If I went back to the states I wouldn't last a single day. Like I said, being married would be unfair to you. Don't you see, I just couldn't subject my family to a life of running and hiding. I'm sorry my love but I can never be married to anyone, not until I cleared myself with the mob. Right now I'm a marked man."

"What do they want, money? I have plenty of money. We could buy them off."

"Thank you for your offer, love. That's not what they want. They want to fulfill their vendetta. They want my hide. The only way this will go away is when their Mafia chief dies and then maybe the mob will forget me. I'm sorry Cathy. We can't get married at this time." This decision ended their relationship. She refused to continue the romance with no future in sight.

Six months later Cathy Sullivan married a wealthy Irishman and the marriage proved to be very fruitful after producing three children, two girls and a boy. Bismarck never went back to Ireland after that. The only two girls he had ever cared for were now both married.

One day Bismarck was in a restaurant in his London hotel by himself when he thought he recognized a woman sitting by herself in an isolated corner. Then he remembered her. It was Angela Wagner, the woman he had jilted of eight hundred grand when he played the part of a minister. He couldn't believe his eyes. Bismarck didn't have a disguise on so he was sure she hadn't detected him. He was wondering if she was there by coincidence or was it another set-up. Lately he wasn't so sure of himself since he found out from Lisa about Mr. Nichols's dedicated revenge to destroy him. Bismarck could have just as easily walked out of that restaurant and disappeared but his quandary was, set-up or not, he couldn't resist a new challenge. He hasn't had any fun since he came to England so he decided to have another crack at her. Hell, what's he got to lose.

He left his table and went back up to his hotel room where he was staying. This time he picked a younger disguise to deceive her. The last time they met he was a man in his forties playing the part of a minister. Now he will play the part of a Scotland Yard Inspector.

Bismarck went back down to the restaurant and stayed in the lobby. From there he could see that she hadn't left and was finishing her dessert. He went right up to her and said, "I beg your pardon, Madam. I'm Inspector Charles Morelly from Scotland Yard. Would you follow me please."

Out in the lobby the inspector said, "I would like to ask you a few questions, if you don't mind."

"Of course, Inspector. What do wish to know and what have I done?"

"Nothing, I'm sure. It's purely a formality. Because of the Hitler situation we are investigating every person that is on vacation here in England. May I see your passport, please... Ah, I see your name is Miss Wagner. Are you here on vacation from Germany?"

"No! Of course not. I'm not German. I'm an American. It just so happens I have a German name but I was born in America and my family dates back to the American revolution, at least on my mother's side."

"Well, you will have to come with me, please. There are still a few questions I must ask you."

Bismarck walked her to his Roll Royce and made her get in. He then drove her to another hotel. When they came into the hotel he had to register for a room as Mr. and Mrs. Wagner. When they entered the room he asked her politely to sit down. He then pretended to make a few phone calls. She was mystified over what was happening to her.

"I'm sorry I have to detain you like this, Miss Wagner, but we must investigate everyone that might be a suspect of being a spy. You understand? You do have a German name so we must check you out. If everything is in order you may go free and continue to enjoy your vacation. May I offer you a drink."

She was even more perplexed and answered, "No thank you. I wish to speak with an attorney if you don't mind."

"Certainly."

Bismarck place another call but this time it was to Wilson. He told John the situation and asked him to send over a crooked mouthpiece that can be trusted. An hour later a man knocked on the door. When he entered he immediately wanted to know where his client was. Bismarck introduced him as Mr. Shepherd, who was regarded as a special councillor for foreign visitors.

Mr. Shepherd first tried to console her. "Miss Wagner. You have no cause to be alarmed. I will straighten out this whole affair in short order. Do you have any other identification other than your passport?"

"No. Not with me. Do I need it?"

"Well, it would have helped. Inspector. I would like to talk to my client in private, if I may."

"Certainly. Take her into the bedroom."

When they were alone the lawyer said to her that the situation looks bad. "My dear. With the Germans on the rampage, England is arresting anyone with the least bit of suspicion. They are corralling any and all people with German names and indiscriminately putting them in jail without even a fair trial. You see, the country is now under Marshal Law and our civil courts are powerless to help any foreign visitors such as yourself.

Angela was getting panicky. "But what can I do? Can't I go to the American Embassy?"

"I'm afraid not. You see, you are now considered a German spy and the United States has no jurisdiction over your case."

"Is there no hope for me at all?"

"Well, yes there is. But I don't know if you can afford it."

"What do you mean?"

"Well, my dear. There is a certain judge that I have dealt with from time to time on similar cases. He is, you might say, a little unscrupulous. To be frank with you, for the right price he could be bought off."

"How much do you think he would accept?"

"I'm afraid it's quite high, on the order of say one hundred thousand American dollars, but in cash."

"Very well, I'll do it, but how can I get the money to him in cash?"

"Very simple. Since the Inspector will not allow you to leave this room at all, you could write me a check for that amount. I will deposit it in my account and after it has cleared through the banks in two days I will draw out the cash and personally give it to the Judge myself. The Judge will proceed to order your release and after that I will escort you to the Queen Mary which is scheduled to leave for America in a few days. You will then be free to go home safely."

Angela Wagner did exactly what the lawyer asked her to do and wrote the check while sitting on the bed. After the lawyer had left, Inspector Morelly came back into the bedroom where she was waiting.

Bismarck notice how pitiful she looked sitting on the bed but that didn't stop him and addressed her sternly, "Miss Wagner. Since you will have to wait for the Judge's orders I suggest that you now take off your clothes."

"What! You must be mad. I refuse."

"Miss Wagner. You have no choice. Either you submit to me voluntarily or I will take you by force. Either way, I will have you." He spoke with extreme authority.

Miss Wagner reluctantly began removing her clothes. The inspector just stood there watching her every move. He was still fascinated over her large bosom. She began crying as she avoided looking at her presumed attacker. She felt so helpless. When she was completely naked the inspector, who was still dressed, walked over to her and stood her up. He put his arms around her and kissed her lips. For a short moment she thought she was being kissed by her former lover, Reverend Jones. His lips were very similar, soft and voluptuous. She closed her eyes and was ready for the worst. The inspector, however, pushed her back onto the bed and unexpectedly walked out of the bedroom. When he didn't return she wasn't sure she should be relieved or disappointed. She quickly put her clothes back on.

Bismarck sometimes just loved to tease his victims. He couldn't help himself. The look on her face was worth more than the money he was extorting from her. He was having such a good time. He knew he had scared the hell out of her and almost gave himself away after he kissed her and laughed out loud. He was tempted to go all the way with her but that would only take the fun of it away.

On her trip back to the States Angela kept to herself. Since the Queen Mary was under British control she didn't want to have anymore trouble. When she finally docked in the states she was met by Mr. Nichols at a pier in New York.

"What happened, Miss Wagner? Did you do as I asked, and were you and Mr. Young able to extort Bismarck as we had planned?"

"No. I was arrested. I didn't even get a chance to meet with Mr. Young. I was at this restaurant waiting for him to arrive when I was detained by a Scotland Yard Inspector. He said because of my German name he had to question me at his hotel for being a possible German spy and......" After Mr. Nichols heard the rest of the story he was furious. He knew now that Bismarck had struck again. All he could say out loud was, "Shit!" and walked away from her without any explanation.

Bismarck continued to live on the interest from his English savings. His money in America, South America and in Switzerland were untouched and were growing rapidly with interest. At this time he was close to being a billionaire and if it were ever known he might be considered one of the richest men in the world.

The only problem he envisioned that might spoil his simple way of life in England was the Axis and the possiblity of war. Mussolini had already conquered Abyssinia in July of 1936 and by November a Rome-Berlin Axis was announced by Mussolini and Hitler. By March of 1939 the Nazis entered Prague, the capital of Czechoslovakia. Hitler was on the move, and by September 1, 1939 the Germans crossed the Polish frontier which caused the British prime minister, Neville Chamberlain, to declare war on Germany on September 3, 1939.

Bismarck was now 36 years old. If America enters the war he could be drafted since the draft age limit was increased to 38. He thought about his situation and decided that if he had to be in the service he wanted to make sure it would be on his terms. He would select the military organization and not be drafted as a common soldier. He always desired to have full control of his own destiny and he certainly didn't like the idea of fighting for any country. With all the money he has accumulated over the years he thought it was about time he put it to some good use, and if necessary he would buy his way into a nice lucrative military assignment.

He asked John and his wife, Mary, to come into the living room. He wanted to discuss a new project with them.

"John and Mary, now that England and France are at war with Germany and Italy, I'm convinced that it won't be too long before the U.S. enters the war. If they do I might be drafted. I think you are safe, John, because you're over 38 and you have a family.

"What I'm proposing now is that we should take advantage of the situation and get into the entertainment and black market business. England will surely be the home base for all American soldiers and they will need to be entertained. Let's face it, if we don't take on this endeavor someone else will. My plan is to first buy a hotel in London and convert it into a casino with live entertainment. It will be called, The Stars and Stripes Palace."

"But Bill. What do we know about show business?" asked John.

"Nothing. Absolutely nothing. But we do know an awful lot

about gambling and how to operate a casino, don't we? Now as far as black market is concerned I have a Canadian friend who is a professional in that department. What I'm proposing to do is have Mary handle the Casino and the live entertainment. We will use the back of the casino as a front for our black market business. My friend's name in Canada is Harry Stark, and he will handle having the goods transported to England from Canada, and you, John, will control the sale of the goods at this end. I will assist you, of course, but should I get involved in the war, you'll have to go it alone.

"We will start by storing non-perishable goods in a warehouse I have already purchased in Scotland, and then we will wait for the right time to sell them. As the goods become scarce we should be able to multiply our investments. As far as the perishable goods are concerned we will sell them as soon as they arrive."

"You think the U.S. will draft you, Bill?"

"I'm not going to wait, John. I want to make sure I get a cushy job and stay right here in England. I already have sent a cable gram to General Burchard in Canada. Stark informs me that the General can be bought off. I may have to enlist in the Canadian Air Corps to avoid the U.S. draft. I do have a pilots license, you know."

Harry Stark was a large man who had served time in two different Canadian prisons for bootlegging liquor to the U.S. during the prohibition era. When Bismarck cabled him he was overjoyed with the prospect of a new business venture because he wasn't doing so well after they repealed prohibition in the United States. The first thing he did was to hire the services of a cargo ship that was docked in Nova Scotia. This particular ship was a converted ocean liner called, The Hudson. The reason he selected this liner was that it could cruise at 30 knots. Speed was essential during the war thus avoiding being torpedoed by those dreaded but slow German U-Boats. With Bismarck's money he was able to purchased many items from the U.S. Some were non-perishable goods such as canned goods, wines, liquor, clothing, and nylon stockings; and other items that were for immediate sale such as sugar, salt, flour, and cigarettes.

In London, it took six months to renovate the hotel Bismarck purchased because material was so scarce. Bismarck had to illegally bring in lumber and material from the states. Transporting goods from Canada wasn't all that easy. Besides avoiding being sunk by the German U-Boats they were having problems with the American authorities. Bismarck's ship was stopped once by an American destroyer and boarded. Their cargo was inspected but since they had no military equipment on board the destroyer's captain released them. His orders did not specify stopping the shipment of non-military goods to England.

On the next trip to England Stark's ship came across a U-Boat. The Germans fired two torpedoes at them but they were able to dodge them. Bismarck figured that the next time they might not be so lucky and decided they needed protection. Unfortunately, he couldn't ask for an American escort to protect his shipments because they were delivering illegal goods and America was not in the war just yet. Bismarck decided to hire a mercenary destroyer from Brazil as an escort. Even though this escort was very expensive for him the revenue worked out quite well. The first four months of income from the black market sales paid for the expenses of the cargo ship and the destroyer. After that it was all profit.

Business was going strong. The Palace was packed every night with English, Scot, Irish and Canadian soldiers. The hidden warehouse in Scotland was full to the brim. Bismarck had to purchase another warehouse to increase their storage capacity because he was delaying the sales of the goods. He was waiting for a better market price.

At the beginning of the year of 1940, Bismarck was still not involved in the war. General Burchard was now permanently assigned to England and made a phone call to Bismarck.

"Mr. Perkins, I understand that you are interested in joining the Canadian Air Corps."

"That's right, General. Why don't you come over to the Palace as my guest and we can discuss it."

When the General entered the Palace a man was waiting for him at the door and escorted him to an upstairs office. Inside he met William Perkins, alias Bismarck Jones.

"Greetings General. Would you care for a drink?"

"Sherry will do fine, thank you. Now what business do you have in mind, Mr. Perkins?"

"Well you see, sir. I'm a very rich man. I can afford just about anything I want here in England and to be blunt, I'm willing to pay out a very large sum to the right person if I could obtain the right position in the military, if you know what I mean."

"Look, Mr. Perkins. Lets not beat around the bush. Mr. Stark has already briefed me about your intentions. You want a high position in the Canadian Air Corps and you are willing to pay for it. What kind of money are we talking about here."

"I can see, General, you like to come right to the point. Well, I admit what you say and to achieve this position I am willing to part with one hundred thousand American dollars."

The general was stunned for a moment. His eyes became wide. The most he had ever received before was ten thousand dollars for the previous times he was on the take from different politicians in Canada. They all wanted him to provide their sons with safe assignments in the service and to stay out of the fighting war. Even that amount was enormous in those days considering the average American worker earned thirty bucks a week.

"Sounds interesting, Mr. Perkins," trying to control his enthusiasm. "It just so happens that I need an assistant here in England which carries the rank of Colonel. I'll be traveling back and forth to Canada and to the United States occasionally, so I will need someone here to represent me while I'm away. If you will accept that position, Mr. Perkins, I promise you you'll never see action on the front."

"Very good, General. I thank you for your offer and I will have our mutual friend in Canada deliver a cashiers check for the amount we discussed to any Canadian bank you choose in your name. Is that satisfactory with you, sir?"

"Yes it is. Thank you. This is the bank you can send it to." He wrote down the bank's name and handed it over to Bismarck.

"You can report to my aide in a week and he will have everything ready for you. You will then be sworn in. You may stay at your present address and commute from there to the Canadian headquarters. You may also call me Pierre if you wish and I will call you Bill. Are we in accord?"

"Yes we are, Pierre. In the meantime you may stay here at the Palace as my permanent guest anytime you choose at my expense of course, and as long as you wish. I'll have a room permanently assigned to you and one of our pretty hostesses will be visiting with you shortly, so please enjoy yourself. Just sign the name General Jones on any tabs presented to you and my people will honor that signature."

"Thank you Bill. I believe I will stay the weekend. I think we're going to make a fine team together." He then left the room and was immediately met by a young lady who was dressed in a very skimpy outfit that exposed much of the white cleavage of her full breast. The general was indeed delighted.

The European Campaign

In the year of 1940, England was deeply involved in the war against the Germans. Colonel Perkins, alias Bismarck Jones, was officially accepted in the Canadian Air Corps as General Burchard's assistant. It was a cushy job for him and he definitely liked the arrangement. He would report to the Canadian Headquarters every day and his duties were simply to act as a figure head and sign requisitions for material. It was the perfect setup he wanted. It kept him away from the fighting war and gave him the freedom to continue to run his casino and black market racket in London without any interference from either government.

When General Burchard went back to Canada, however, Bismarck was put in charge of the Canadian Air force stationed in England. This sort of disturbed him. First of all, he didn't care who won the war and second he didn't know anything about running the Canadian Air Corps. He was becoming a little sorry that he had agreed to be the general's assistant because he now had to go to all of those officer's meetings and listen to all of that strategy crap. He was being put in a position where he had to make military decisions that could affect the lives of many Canadian pilots. He also had to go to the English Headquarters and listen to those old fat English generals brag about how they won the first world war. As far as Bismarck was concerned, they didn't know beans about this modern warfare. He was getting bored with the whole affair or worst, frustrated.

Something then happened that disturbed him even more. While he was listening to a plan being presented by the commanding officer, General Hollingsworth, Bismarck didn't particularly like the precarious position the Canadian bomber pilots were being assigned. The general had the Canadian pilots flying without a fighter escort toward Hamburg while the English bombers that were flying toward Berlin had several British fighters escorting them most of the way into Germany. The British Spitfires did not have the range to fly all the way to

Berlin and back unless they carried extra petro onboard or refueled themselves in an isolated area some where in France.

Bismarck couldn't stand being quiet any longer and stood up to be recognized. "General Hollingsworth, sir. Why is it that the Canadians do not have a proper escort for this upcoming raid?"

"Colonel Perkins, I would like to provide you with an escort but we have a limited number of fighters for this mission and the Berlin raid will attract more enemy resistance from German fighters. The Germans will attempt to protect their capital more than they would Hamburg. They have a very large defensive squadron of fighters in Berlin to protect their capital."

Bismarck was becoming furious, "I'm sorry, general, but I cannot subject my men in a raid that would be just plain suicide. I must insist that you provide some protection or I will have to transfer our own fighters that are now being deployed for defensive purposes to protect London from German attack."

"Colonel, you will be disobeying a direct order. General Burchard and I have already agreed with this plan and now you wish to change it?"

Bismarck's mind was working fast. His Con capabilities were traveling through his mind. It's the same old story. Make them a sucker's deal and they can't wait to climb on board.

"I tell you what, General. If you will permit me to use my fighters as an escort for our bombers I will personally deliver to you twenty American made P-47 fighters in one month."

"And how do you propose to do that. We've been trying to get American fighters delivered here for six months now, and we still do not have a one."

"I repeat, sir, I will personally guarantee this delivery or I will pay the cost for the first five P-47s myself. Do we have a deal?"

"Colonel, you must be out of your mind..." The General then sat back in his chair and thought it over a bit. He had heard about this Colonel Perkins and his black-market trade which the British allowed as long as he was somehow bringing American goods to England. He had a hunch, "You know, Colonel. I think I'll take a chance on you. I'll agree to your terms, but if you fail on this promise you will never get me to agree on anything else again.

Understood?"

"Yes sir."

And so, without Bismarck realizing it, he was now getting involved in the war. He certainly didn't want to, but after sitting through so many poorly planed maneuvers he was getting perplex and had to do something. After this arrangement he no longer will be able to act as a silent officer.

When he left General Hollingsworth's meeting he sent a message to Harry Stark in Canada to purchase these fighters. Stark was completely puzzled by this latest request. How will he be able to purchase twenty P-47 Thunderbolt fighters made by Republic. He decided to make a few phone calls to some friends in New York and after contriving all kinds of deals and promises two weeks later a cargo transport pulled into the Nova Scotia harbor in Canada from the States. The ship unloaded twenty P-47 airplanes on the dock. After another two weeks they reappeared again in a Scotland port and were later delivered by train directly to the Royal Air Corps base outside of London in care of General Hollingsworth. The only problem with the exchange was that the General had to pay a premium price for the American fighters, but it was worth it. Bismarck didn't have to cough up a dime. He actually made a million pounds on the deal.

"How did Colonel Perkins get them, General?" asked his aide.

"I don't know how he did it and I'm not going to ask either." The General immediately signed the receipt for the goods and as a result of this devious proposal England was able to receive its first shipment of American fighters.

It turned out that Republic had originally over produced P-47 fighters. They had speculated that the war in Europe would expand and the U.S. would become involved. Republic took a chance and expected the U.S. Air Corps to purchase them not only for England but for themselves. As a result thirty surplus planes were available and were sitting in hangers waiting for a buyer. The sale of twenty planes to the Canadian Air Corps was a welcome relief. Republic didn't know that Stark was not a representative of the Canadian Air Corps and they didn't bother to check his credentials, either. The sale was made without the U.S. Government's knowledge and it helped Republic overcome some of its financial loses. Many American companies were selling arms to England under the table at the time and President Roosevelt purposely ignored these trades. He actually wanted to help England in any way he could as long the U.S. Government wasn't directly involved. The American public was against getting involved in the war so it was a touchy subject at the White House.

The next time Bismarck met with General Hollingsworth another military subject came up. This time it was military clothing, blankets, tooth paste, medical supplies, and spare parts for the American fighters he had just purchased.

Bismarck then sent another cable to Stark in Canada ordering him to hire another fast cargo ship. It seems selling to the military was becoming more profitable than his black market business. One of the most lucrative products sold to the Royal Air Corps was American cigarettes. For every dollar Bismarck spent on cigarettes his black market business grossed four dollars in return from the military.

Later on, Bismarck was introduced to Admiral Jennings of the Royal Navy and General Cummings of the British Army by General Hollingsworth. Both the admiral and the general were exceptionally fond of American cigars and Port wines. With their additional orders of goods for the Royal Army and Navy, Bismarck threw in free cigars and cases of Port wine for them to use personally.

The Admiral later came to Bismarck's office to order a new shipment. The discussion somehow drifted to American Indians. "You know Perkins. I have never met an American Indian. I've read so much about them and I must say I've develop a special fondness for them, especially their squaws. Isn't that how one calls their women?"

Bismarck was thinking fast. "Yes it is, Admiral. Let me ask you, sir, have you ever attended my Palace?"

"No. I can't say that I have."

"Well then, it just so happens that a full blooded American Indian squaw is on her way to work for me as a hostess in the

Palace to provide a diversion for the troops. She should arrive in a week and, with your permission, I will be happy to introduce her to you. I will personally see to it that she shall provide entertainment only for you, exclusively."

"Perkins. You are a devil. By God, I must say, I will certainly be looking forward to meeting her. Thanks again for everything and, by the way, I have just decided to double the shipment I just gave you."

Bismarck laughed to himself, "The old dog is a pervert. I'll fix his ass and take all the business he can throw my way." Bismarck sent another unusual message to Stark who then placed a young Sioux Squaw prostitute from South Dakota on his cargo ship that was headed for Scotland to provide special services for Admiral Jennings at the Palace. It's business as usual.

The prosperous arrangement for Bismarck went on for the next year until finally the U.S. entered the war on Germany. Bismarck then tried to convert all of his profits into American dollars because he was leery of the English pound as inflation was jumping rapidly in England. This introduced another problem for him since he wasn't paying American taxes. He then decided to transfer two million dollars in securities to a Swiss bank to hide some of his assets. He couldn't trust anyone to accomplish this task so he decided to do it himself. He discovered there was a secret mission involving a cargo plane that periodically flies to Switzerland once a week. Bismarck made arrangements to go along with this aircraft and make his own personal deposit in a Swiss bank. On this one flight there was a special emissary of English brass aboard whose main mission was to borrow a sizable amount of money from a major Swiss bank to help England finance the war effort.

It was in the winter of 1942 when a cargo plane carrying four military men and one civilian took off for Switzerland from London. Bismarck was the only man in civilian clothes who was impersonating a business man with forged papers. As the plane entered the Swiss boarder on it's way to Geneva, a German Messerschmitt came swooping down from behind and opened fired on them. One of the two plane's engines had stopped as a result of the gunfire and without warning the engine burst into flames. The pilot announced to all passengers to secure their parachutes and be prepared to jump. When the plane passed over the Swiss boarder the German fighter left them to their doom. The English pilot was hoping to land in Geneva with one engine, but he lost his bearings and didn't know where he was. He actually by-passed Geneva and was heading for the Italian boarder, but then all of a sudden the wing with the bad engine was also on fire and began to disintegrate. He gave the orders to abandon the aircraft and one by one the five passengers and the copilot bailed out.

As Bismarck was floating down he looked up waiting for the pilot to bail out but then there was a mighty explosion from the airplane with the captain still in it. He never made it out of the cockpit.

Bismarck and the others drifted down to a valley in the Alps. As they landed in the rough terrain one of the passengers broke his leg. The copilot was killed as he landed into an open crevice and was buried in a deep snow drift. The passenger with the broken leg was a French Major who was on a special mission to transport secret papers to the French Embassy in Geneva. They quickly buried their parachutes in the snow and made a stretcher for the Frenchman. The British colonel took charge and decided they should all head east. Bismarck, who was familiar with this area, said that the best way to go would be to the west but he was overruled. So he just tagged along. They had a better chance of surviving if they stuck together, he thought.

The region was mountainous and very difficult to maneuver in, especially carrying a man on a makeshift stretcher. In the meantime, the Frenchman was losing blood and he knew that he could not continue this journey with them. When they stopped for a break the Frenchman asked to speak with Bismarck. He spoke in French which Bismarck understand.

"My friend, I know that I cannot make this journey in the condition I'm in. I'm bleeding badly and I am just holding you up. You must leave me here and save yourselves."

"Nonsense. We will not go another step without you," replied Bismarck. The other three men didn't care one way or another what happened to the Frenchman.

"He's right you know," said the English courier whose main job was to obtain the loan from the Swiss bank at any cost. Nothing else mattered to him and nothing was going to stop him from his mission of obtaining that loan. His one partner agreed and they both headed out leaving Bismarck and the navigator MacBain, a Scot, to carry the Frenchman. They picked up the crude stretcher with the Frenchman and continued their slow journey. Nightfall arrived and, by now, they lost sight of the other Englishmen who were moving at a faster pace. Worst of all, the winds picked up momentum reducing the chill factor to minus 40 degrees Fahrenheit. They decided to take shelter beside a cliff that would provide them some protection from the weather. The Frenchman again pleaded with Bismarck to leave him there.

"My friend. You must leave me or you will all perish." Bismarck ignored him.

"Promise me one thing Mr. Perkins. If I should die, will you take this briefcase to the French Embassy in Geneva? It is vital that you do this for me."

"You are not going to die. I have stopped the bleeding now and I'm sure you will survive, but just in case, I promise to deliver your package."

That night they were cuddled up close to each other to keep warm but all of a sudden Bismarck woke up to the crack of a gun shot. He looked over at the Frenchman and saw that he had shot himself. Now Bismarck had no choice but to fulfill his promise to the dead Frenchman.

Bismarck was familiar with the area having skied in Switzerland many times. He knew that the Englishmen's trip east would be impossible and to go west would be safer. He also knew that there were rescue stations toward the west of this location which the Swiss purposely installed at specific sites for such emergencies. The Scot was completely against going west and preferred to join the English, so they decided to split up. The next morning the Scot headed in the same direction he thought the Englishmen were headed. Bismarck knew that they would never survive and right now his only concerned was saving himself. The first thing he did was remove the clothes from the dead Frenchman before he buried him in the snow. He may need them for himself later, he thought.

The trip was grueling as he had to climb steep hills and maneuver down sheer ravens through the deep snow. At one point he had to sit down on the snow to slide down a deep embankment. By the time he reached the bottom he was completely soaking wet and he knew by night fall his clothes would freeze solid which wouldn't protect him from the cold. He started gathering wood and started a fire between two heavy boulders. He took his clothes off and replaced them with the Frenchman's. He made a roof of sticks and loose logs and put his own cloths on top to protect him from any new snow. He was now secure for the night but he didn't have any food left. It began snowing again and this time it was a major blizzard. All he could do was wait it out.

The next morning when the snow subsided Bismarck discovered he was completely buried in a snow drift. He had to push at the snow with his legs to open a hole. He began to panic a little but then he finally saw daylight. He was relieved. Bismarck was now becoming very distressed as he looked at the never ending snow ahead. He always had control of his destiny but now it seemed hopeless. He started out again and began talking to himself to pass the time to avoid the inevitable.

"Yes sir. Tomorrow I'll be eating venison and sitting by a fireplace nice and warm. Yes sir." He was acting a bit delirious.

He walked for the next four hours and all a sudden in the distance he saw smoke rising to the heavens. He was getting excited and began to run in that direction. The snow was becoming deeper and seriously reduced his progress. Every so often, he would fall into a deep hole and had difficulty climbing out. He was now exhausted and had to rest occasionally. He would just sit on the snow to relax and was determined not allow the environment engulf him. Slowly he approached the origin of the smoke. He saw that it was coming from a cabin on a hill top. He began yelling as loud as he could. He took his pistol out and fired a shot in the air. A man opened the door of the cabin looked around the area and finally saw him. He came down to him as fast as he could and assisted Bismarck back up to the cabin.

Bismarck was saved.

In the cabin the man spoke in perfect Italian, "Sir, we do not exchange names here. Because of the war there are all kinds of people escaping through these mountains. To protect ourselves we just help one another and ask no questions."

That assertion was no problem for Bismarck. Now that he is eating solid food he could care less who his rescuer was. "I agree. It is a smart thing to do," he replied.

Bismarck still had the Frenchman's brief case tied to his belt and the man didn't question him about it, either. To Bismarck, the man's Italian was not normal sounding. The accent was more of a class room learning type. Too perfect. Bismarck figured he was not Italian but had learned it at a school in another country, probably Germany. He was probably a Jew trying to escape to Switzerland.

The man then asked, "Are you familiar with this area?"

"Yes I am. I was heading for Geneva when my car broke down. I thought I could make it across the valley but the snow was too deep. I do know where most of these shelters are located so I thought I could survive the trip."

The stranger said, "I have been here for four days now waiting for the storm to subside, but I don't know which way to go from here."

"When I get a little stronger, maybe by tomorrow, I will guide you," said Bismarck. The man seemed pleased.

The man had shot a deer and cooked it a few days ago. There was no other food in the cabin. Bismarck assessed the amount that was left and figured that there would be enough to get them to the next shelter. Usually, there is plenty of canned goods in these shelters but it was obvious that this one had no provisions left. He hoped the next station still had food in it. Sometimes, hunters would eat the food even though it was for emergency purposes only. The food was especially stored in these stations with the intentions of feeding desperately lost skiers and hunters.

The man was well armed with a rifle and two pistols. Bismarck had only the one pistol on him and he began having suspicions about the man. First, he didn't look Jewish at all and second, he acted too much like a military man. Over the many years as a hustler, Bismarck learned the habits of people from different countries and from his past experiences he did not trust this one. He figured that once he guides this man out of the mountains and eventually to the last station he wouldn't put two cents on his own life. That evening he check out his own pistol replace the bullet he wasted and was ready. Bismarck estimated that there were at least four more shelters before they would reach Geneva. Once the man is sure he can make it on his own at that last station, he will undoubtedly make his move.

The Swiss had set the distances between shelters so that it would take one days walk through heavy snow to reach the next shelter and avoid an overnight stay in the dark. Fortunately, in each of the shelters they reached there was plenty of food, and the danger of starving to death was over. They stayed two nights at each station before they went on. After a week of traveling they finally came to the last station. Bismarck sensed that the man is aware of this fact. He began acting jolly and removed a bottle of schnapps that was stored in his pack. He broke it out and offered Bismarck a drink. He was celebrating. Maybe Bismarck was being too cautious. The man was definitly overjoyed and didn't appear to be a killer.

The next morning he told Bismarck to lead the way. Up until then the stranger was always in the lead, turning around periodically to insure that he was going in the right direction. Bismarck would always point the way to the next shelter. Bismarck knew now that it was time for the assassination to take place and he removed his right glove so that his trigger finger would be ready. As they rounded a bend in the hills he heard the sudden noise of a bolt action from behind him. He quickly turned and saw that the stranger had placed the rifle butt against his right shoulder and was raising the barrel towards him. Bismarck immediately whirled and pulled out his pistol and shot the man between the eyes. He then walked over to the man lying in the snow. He was curious about this man and opened his heavy fur coat. Underneath his coat was a German uniform. Bismarck was sort of puzzled because he thought it was such a waste. Why was this guy out here in no man's land in the first place? It was certainly a mystery to him. Unknown to Bismarck, however, the

German was purposely stationed there to detain any Jewish refuges that were escaping to Switzerland. He was to capture them and wait for assistance to bring them back to Germany.

Bismarck finally arrived in Geneva and headed for a hotel. Of all the deals he ever pulled, he was sure that this one would have been his downfall. But lady luck was on his side once again. He went to the first hotel he saw and stumbled in. He had Swiss currency with him and paid for their most expensive suite. He took a hot bath and remained in it for hours until he was sure he had thawed out. That night he slept like a log.

The next morning he headed for the Swiss Bank where he had his holdings and was able to deposit his securities with no trouble. He then went to the French Embassy and gave the briefcase to the French Ambassador. The Ambassador thanked him over and over again. Bismarck didn't know what was in the briefcase because it was in code. He had already looked and couldn't make heads or tails out of it. It turned out to be an important document describing the location of French freedom fighters and a plan to attack a German convoy carrying military equipment that was on its way to France through Switzerland. The Ambassador called Bismarck a hero. Bismarck just grinned and departed. His only thoughts right now was to go back to England, but he had to make one more stop. He headed for the Swiss main headquarters.

In German, Bismarck spoke to the Swiss Interior of business affairs, Hans Spelling. "Sir, I'm Colonel Perkins and I'm here representing the English Government. It is my task to appropriate a loan from you that will be used in the war effort for England. Are you aware of this transaction, sir?"

"Yes I am, but I was supposed to deal with a Colonel Wright. What happened to him?"

"Sir, we were shot down over your country by the Germans and I'm afraid Mr. Wright and his party all perished in the snow carrying the important documents with him from King George. I'm the only survivor left. If you will give me the loan and a flight back to England I will see to it that the money goes the king. You may radio the British and ask for General Hollingsworth. He will verify my position."

"Very well, Mr. Perkins. After I make the radio call in code I will give you five million pounds to be delivered directly to the king himself. I will then provide you with a plane and an escort of two of my men to assure that the transaction takes place. The briefcase containing the bonds will be hand-cuffed to your left wrist. Only one of the men escorting you will have the key to the handcuffs and the other has the key to open the pad lock on the briefcase. This way we will be absolutely sure it doesn't get into the wrong hands. You see, anyone can convert these bonds into cash. Are there any questions, Mr. Perkins?"

There was non, so after he was cleared by General Hollingsworth, Bismarck and his two companions were taken to the Geneva airport and placed on a Swiss plane headed for England. Because of severe weather that day and to avoid German fighters, a round about flight was taken. It took eight hours instead of three to fly to London but they landed without a hitch.

Bismarck and his companions were immediately ushered into a Rolls Royce and driven to Buckingham Palace. They were then escorted directly to King George VI. In the kings presence one of the Swiss escorts removed the handcuffs from Bismarck and placed the briefcase on a small table next to the kings side. The other escort then unlocked the padlock that secured the briefcase and stepped aside. A very old man walked up to it, opened the briefcase and removed its contents. The bonds were in increments of one hundred thousand pounds apiece and he began counting them out. When he was finished he slowly walked over to the king and whispered something in his ear. The king then looked down at Bismarck who was standing nonchalantly in front of him not paying much attention to what was going on.

"Mr. Perkins, are you aware that there is a 100,000 pound note missing from this briefcase?"

"No, your highness. As you can see there was a lock on the briefcase and it is completely tamper proof. No one could have possibly gotten into it."

The king asked the Swiss escorts, "Did anyone meddled with this briefcase, gentleman?"

"No, your highness. We were constantly on guard. We alternated shifts in sleeping to make sure that no one tampered with it."

The king had his suspicions and ordered Bismarck to be searched. They found nothing. Either the Swiss councillor short changed him or this man is a crook. He couldn't see how Perkins could steal the bond, but then again he did put his life on the line for England and if he did manage to bring the money. It was well worth it. He dismissed him but immediatly called for his minister of security.

"I want that man, Perkins, completely checked out. I want to know all about him even down to what type of shorts he wares. Understood?"

Bismarck could never resist the temptation of an easy heist. That security lock was child's play for him. He was tempted to take more than the one hundred thousand pound note but then he figured 4.9 million pounds for England should satisfy the king. Why be greedy? Bismarck didn't need the money, but the temptation of getting away with a heist right from under their noses was so overwhelming, he couldn't resist it. He finally went back to his own Palace and was met by John and his wife, Mary.

John spoke to him first. "Bismarck, where the devil were you? You said you had business to attend to but said nothing about Switzerland. What Happened?"

"The least you both know the better. Look at this, I just made a hundred thousand pounds just by flying from Switzerland back to England," he said with a broad grin. "The reason I went to Switzerland in the first place was to deposit some of our money in a Swiss bank. I opened up an account for both of you and deposited a million dollars worth of securities for you. If we lose the war you will both be financially secure. Naturally, I deposited the same amount in my account." He handed their Swiss bank statements to Mary to store in their safety deposit box.

The next day Bismarck received a call from the Ambassador of France. "Monsieur Perkins. Will you do me the honor of attending a party at the French Embassy. The French Government wants to thank you for your effort in bringing those important papers to the French freedom fighters. The outcome proved to be very successful as we were able to destroy a German convoy when it entered France through Switzerland."

"Thank you very much, sir. I will be happy to attend."

That evening the French Ambassador bestowed upon Bismarck the French Cross medal of Honor to show their appreciation for his heroic effort in helping France in their underground war resistance. At the affair Bismarck met a beautiful French secretary. He thought maybe she came with the award but it turned out to be only a one night stand because her husband was expected to arrive soon after fighting for a year in France in the underground movement. Bismarck didn't care. He accepted any gifts bestowed on him, no questions asked.

When Bismarck reported to headquarters again, General Hollingsworth questioned him on why he went to Switzerland in the first place, without his permission.

"My orders came directly from General Burchard himself, to make contact with the Canadian Embassy there. I'm sorry, but I didn't have time to brief you. I just barely made the flight out on time." None of this was true, of course, but Bismarck needed an excuse. He could only hope that the General did not beforehand make contact with Burchard.

"Very well, Bill. But next time please inform me of any more orders you receive from Burchard."

"I will, sir." He was relieved.

As he walked out of the generals office he met Admiral Jennings. They talked briefly about different things but then Bismarck asked, "By the way, sir. Has Miss Clearwater arrived from America yet?"

"Yes she has, Bill. I do appreciate what you have done for me. She is a lovely girl. I can't believe how experienced she is at only sixteen years of age. She's great."

Bismarck grinned to himself and thought that these new games he's playing are getting to be more fun than gambling and swindling. He then excused himself and headed back to the Palace.

He didn't originally want to ask the general for permission to go to Switzerland because he knew he would have been turned down. He had to get that money into Switzerland at any cost because he was sure, at that time, that the Germans would win the war. He decided that America was too busy making Cadillacs and their entering the war wouldn't change the outcome. Bismarck was convinced that Hitler was too strong and eventually will rule the world, so he had to diversify his savings to a neutral country.

Meantime, Bismarck was content at the way things were going along. He was making money at the casino, the black-market, and the military equipment he was selling to the British. The gambling tables were rigged so that the house would always make a substantial profit. The entertainment costs were just breaking even but Bismarck didn't care. Money was rolling in from all different directions. He was not lacking for anything. He dined well and had several girlfriends that he had met at the Palace who were available to satisfied his sexual desires. Every once in awhile he would think about Countess Lisa and how she was doing in Italy. He then removed her from his mind. She's probably fat as a cow by now as many Italian women get after having a dozen kids and they would be yelling and screaming, he reasoned.

One evening, a well dress man showed up at the Roulette wheel. He was playing high stakes and winning. John called Bismarck in his office to come into to the casino and watch the betting. Bismarck thought he recognized the man but he wasn't sure. He continued to watch and then he spotted it. The dealer was crooked and he was allowing this man to win. The stranger was already one hundred thousand pounds ahead so Bismarck walked over and closed the table.

"What do you mean the table is closed? What kind of a cheap outfit is this?"

Bismarck then immediately recognized the man as Pietro Columbo from New York. They looked at each other for awhile and then Pietro broke the spell with a grin. Bismarck knew why he was here. It was for his hide. It's payback time. He quickly looked around and saw ten men hanging around and knew that Pietro had his henchmen with him.

"Okay. You may continue to play but the new dealer will be

John here." He whispered to John to fire that dealer the first chance he could. He told him the dealer was crooked. Pietro then realized that Bismarck was wise to the set-up so he walked away from the table with the grin still on his face.

Bismarck was aware that Pietro's men would make an attempt on his life that evening so he called to John to come to his office.

"What's up, Bill?"

"Didn't you recognize that gentleman at the table? It's Pietro Columbo, the Mafioso."

"You're right. Oh my gosh, what are you going to do?"

"I hate to say this, John, but I'm going to have to get back to the base and remain there for protection. There is no way his men will be able to get at me at the Canadian Air Corps base, that's for sure. I'm going to change my assignment to the combat team and take over that division. In this way I won't have to leave the base to attend all of those dumb meetings. I don't see any other way out.

"His goons will have me dead in an hour if I stayed here. However, I had prepared for such an emergency. I'm sure by now he has all of the exits covered, but there is an elevator in the basement that I had especially installed when I bought this place. It leads out to the back of the building. The elevator will rise up through the sidewalk and I'll be on it. Have a car sent around there in an hour for me, will you John? The Palace is now your full responsibility."

"Okay, boss. I'll take care of everything and I'll save your share of the profits."

John Wilson decided to bring the car around the back himself. He wanted to make sure no one else knows about Bismarck leaving, but what he didn't know was that one of Pietro's men followed him. His second mistake was to wait for Bismarck in the car. It would have been better if he left the car with the keys in it and went back to the front of the Palace, this way the tail would have followed him back.

The elevator began rising out of the sidewalk and sure enough Bismarck was on it and nonchalantly walked out onto the sidewalk. He saw the car sitting across the street but then he noticed that John was behind the wheel. He first ran across the street to try to warn John to get the hell out of there. He was too late. Sub-machine gun fire came from different directions. They were shooting at Bismarck who kept on running and was able to hide on the opposite side of the vehicle. The gun shots penetrating through the car's front door struck John. Bismarck peaked over the door and saw him slumped over. He was sure he was dead.

He then ran as fast as he could down the street, dodging bullets as he ran from side to side as a halfback would in a football game while trying to avoid being tackled. He managed to turn the corner and found protection in a recessed store entrance. He stayed there for awhile waiting with his own gun in his hand. He saw two men running down the street in his direction. Bismarck wasn't going to wait to see if they were friend or foe. He opened fired at them both and they fell to ground dead. Bismarck saw his chance and ran to a cab that was parked fifty yards away. He ran as fast as he could and without any hesitation he jumped into the cab.

"Get moving!" he yelled. The cab driver immediately took off and Bismarck once again escaped from the Mafia.

At the Canadian Air Corps base Bismarck called Mary. "Mary. This is Bill. I'm sorry to have to tell you this but something terrible has happened. John is dead."

"Oh no." She began crying. After awhile she composed herself and asked, "What happened, Bill?"

"I'm sorry, Mary, but it was those damn New York gangsters that were after me. I don't know if John had told you why I was on the run but it was because the New York Mafia wanted me dead. They got John instead. Mary, you'll have to run the Casino by yourself now. I will send another gentleman over to help run the black-market ring. I'm going to remain here on the base. It's the only safe place for me. Take care of yourself, Mary and I'm deeply sorry. I will keep in touch. Bye."

He then sent a cable to Stark in Canada to come to England with the next shipment. Even though Bismarck didn't particularly like Stark as a friend, he had no choice but to have him take over the English operation.

America Declares War

On December 7, 1941, The Japanese bombed Pearl Harbor in the Hawaiian Islands, and President Roosevelt declared war on Japan and shortly thereafter Germany and Italy declared war on America. England could now receive assistance directly from the U. S. This would put a damper on Bismarck's racket.

Now that America is in the war Bismarck Jones felt fairly safe from the Mafia. As long as he remained within the Canadian Air Corps headquarters he would be well protected and untouchable. To be sure of his safety he had himself assigned to the fighter squadron. He no longer had to leave the base for meetings and be exposed to the mob. It was rather ironic at this point because he didn't want anything to do with the war and now, all of a sudden, here he is in the middle of it all.

General Burchard paid him a visit one day. "Colonel Perkins. I thought you were looking for a cushy job. Now you want to participate in the war. What changed your mind."

"Well, sir. Now that the U.S. is involved I feel I must also become involved. I still love my country, you know." Bismarck lied. He never loved anything or anyone, except maybe Lisa who was now married and a mother. He was, at this point of his life, a completely selfish man and was only looking out for himself.

"That's an outstanding outlook, Bill. I'm extremely proud of you. And because of this new attitude I'm now putting you in charge of the whole squadron. This means, of cause, that you will have to fly on several dangerous missions yourself."

"I'm well prepared to do my duty, sir."

"Good show, Bill. That's the spirit we need to beat those blasted Jerries." They shook hands and the General left.

Bismarck sat there for some time contemplating how he got himself into this mess. He could care less who won the war. Throughout his life his only concern was about himself. Somehow, he's going to have to use his devious mind to get himself out of this outfit. Maybe go to South America. He could live very comfortably there where he still has a sizeable savings. It's an interesting thought but he didn't dare leave the facilities.

Now that he has full authority of the squadron he decided to have a meeting with all the Canadian pilots. At least he wanted to start on the right foot with them.

"Gentleman. I'm Colonel Perkins, your knew commanding officer. I must admit that I don't know too much about your operation but I'm willing to learn. I understand we have thirty fighters in this squadron but not all of them are being used. What, may I ask, is the problem?"

One Lieutenant stood up and said, "Sir. There's just one basic problem. Spare parts. We just don't have enough. The only way we can keep what few planes we have afloat is to cannibalize from the others. This leaves us with only half a squadron operational."

"How come. Aren't the English supplying you with enough parts?" demanded Bismarck.

"That's very simple, sir. We are Canadians. We have no pull in the Royal British Air Corps. We are last on the list for anything, and yet they give us some of the most dangerous assignments. The British still consider Canada a colony with little or no say so in this war."

"Very well, then. I now understand the situation and my first task will be to remedy it. You are all dismissed. I'll take it from here, and believe me, something will be done."

Bismarck first placed a call to General Hollingsworth. "Sir. I want you to know that I have just volunteered myself as the Canadian Fighter squadron commander. When I got here, however, I discovered that we have a definite shortage of spare parts for our fighters. I know you must keep your own fighters in readiness to protect England from attack but I would like to make another deal with you for parts. What I'm offering you now is, I will supply you with a shipment of complete spare parts for your new P-47 fighters, free of charge, in exchange for a complete shipment of spare parts for our thirty Spitfires."

"You got a deal, Colonel. When will I get my parts?"

"You will have them in two weeks, sir."

"In that case, you will have your parts in three weeks, right after ours arrive."

"That'll be fine, sir. Thank you."

Bismarck then hung up smiling. He just enjoys the game of wheeling and dealing. He knows he's going to take a financial hit on this deal so to make up for it he called Mary and told her the minute Stark arrives have him start selling off half of the goods from the first warehouse in Scotland. He then sent another cable to Stark's replacement in Canada, a Mr. Samuel (Sam), to purchase a complete set of spare parts to cover the twenty planes that were sent to England. By the end of the month the Canadian Air Corps had all thirty fighters operational with plenty of replacement parts in storage. The Canadian pilots and crew were delighted with their new commanding officer.

"How do you suppose he did it, Harry?" asked one pilot.

"I don't know," replied Harry. "I understand he has a knack of wheeling and dealing. Not only has he gotten us our spare parts but we now have free cigarettes. I'm certainly glad he's our new commanding officer."

Bismarck decided to lead the next bomber escort over Germany. There were twenty bombers in the mission with both British and Canadian pilots. These will be escorted by six British and four Canadian fighters. The destination is Berlin. The escorts will have to refuel in France to get back to England. The bombers took off first from an English base near Scotland and the Canadian fighters met them halfway across the English Channel. It was to be a night raid and the bombers were depending on the fighters to protect them from enemy fighter attack. As they approached Berlin there was ground flack from all directions. One of the Bombers was hit and the crew had to bailed out. Then Bismarck announced to his fighters, "The Jerries are on their way up. Be prepared men and keep in a tight formation. Good hunting."

The Canadians were great fighters but the new German Messerschmitts were far superior than the Spitfires. The dog fighting was brutal and the Allies lost two more bombers and five fighters of which two were Canadians. The raid was, however, considered a complete success but very costly. Bismarck, himself, shot down three Messerschmitts, but was wounded in the left leg and his plane was in bad shape. He first landed in France to refuel and then limped back to England but had to crash land in a wheat farm. He and his squadron received a commendation directly from Churchill by telephone.

Bismarck spent the next two days in a hospital and was able to make friends with a married nurse. After he was discharged from the hospital she invited him to her flat for dinner. Bismarck brought over a bottle of wine and a pair of nylon stockings. One thing led to another and they eventually ended up in her bed. She was hungry for sex since there was now a major shortage of men in England. The affair was perfect and Bismarck was now satisfied with the arragement. He needed a girlfriend.

When he left her flat, however, a man jumped him in the street. The man came down on him with a knife but Bismarck was able to grab his arm before the knife penetrated his chest. Bismarck then removed a gun from his back holster and shot the man in the stomach. The man simply slumped down to the pavement and slowly died. Bismarck wasn't going to wait around to see who else was involved so he ran to his car and took off. He never went back to visit that nurse again for fear of his own life. So much for having a steady girlfriend. He knows that the Mafia is relentless and they will never give up until they have their vendetta. Somehow Bismarck is going to have to buy off Pietro, or he will be on the run the rest of his life. Right now he is sorry he tangled with them in the first place.

His next mission was to bomb Munich in Bavaria. This time ten bombers were deployed and only five fighters were assigned as escorts. It was another night raid and again the fighting was brutal and the loses were heavy. This raid was also considered successful, even though five bombers were shot down they were able to drop their bombs ahead of time causing severe damage to the factories in the city of Munich. Only one fighter returned to England, however, and Bismarck's plane was not the one. His Spitfire was so badly damaged there was no way he could make it back to England. He was again wounded but this time it was in the left shoulder.

Bismarck decided that the safest place for him to fly was Switzerland, but he was losing control of his aircraft and didn't know exactly where he was. He was bleeding badly and the plane had drifted toward Italy. He saw a lake and thought it was located in Switzerland and began feeling better. He certainly didn't want to be captured by the Germans. His plane began vibrating badly and soon might fall apart so he descended slowly. He decided the safest place to land would be on the water and hope for the best. He didn't know it but the body of water was lake Como in northern Italy. Unfortunately, he came down too fast and when the plane hit the water he was knocked unconscious from the impact.

Even though it was dark a lone fisherman saw his plane crash into the water and he rowed out to rescue the pilot. Shortly thereafter Bismarck was removed from the wreckage by the fisherman and then the plane began to take on water. It finally sank into the deepest part of the lake destroying all evidence that an aircraft was ever there. As the fishing's boat was being rowed away Bismarck opened his eyes momentarily and was able to see his plane sink. He then fell back into a deep coma.

Five days later Bismarck woke up in a strange bed. An old lady asked him in Italian if he was alright. Bismarck answered her in his rather poor Italian, that he was fine. He sat up and asked her where they were.

"This city is called Cernobbio. We are located on the southern tip of Lago Como. Now, no more talking. You must eat and get strong."

Fortunately, these poor Italian peasants didn't know where he came from or who he was. Since he was always in civilian clothing when he was in combat they just assumed that he was a German pilot who crashed into the lake as many German planes have done before. When they asked him if he was German, Bismarck went along and said he was. Bismarck always wore civilian clothes just in case he got shot down in Germany. He figured he could Con himself out of any situation that presented itself as long as he was not in uniform.

After a few days Bismarck thanked them for saving his life and headed south to Milan which was approximately twenty miles away. He hitched a ride on a hay wagon over half the distance but had to walk the rest of the way. He was still weak from the crash and had to stop several times off the road to rest. He finally came across an Inn and headed for it. He had no money on him because it was standard practice for him not to carry English or American money just in case he was shot down over enemy territory. This way, he could then pass himself off as one of the local inhabitants. He was the only Canadian pilot who wore civilian clothing on a mission. Because he could speak several languages he was prepared to play the part of one of the locals if it became necessary. Bismarck certainly didn't want to have to use the Geneva convention rules of war and be buried in a prisoner of war camp in Germany. As a civilian, he figured, he had a better chance of surviving.

Bismarck entered the Inn and noticed that there were two German officers sitting at one of the tables in the restaurant section of the Inn. When he was with the Italians he easily got away with passing himself off as a German, but he was afraid that his German may not be good enough to fool these officers, so he immediately went back out the door.

In his old gambling days, when he had spent several months vacationing in the ski slopes near Munich, he picked up their local accent and learned to speak their dialect very fluently. He could easily pass himself off as a Bavarian, but in this situation he wasn't quite ready to test his accent. German came easy for him because his mother was German born and she often spoke to him in the Bavarian vernacular. His father was the typical American who had a mixture of several nationalities. His father's ancestral background consisted mainly of English, Scot, and some Dutch.

Outside of the Inn he noticed a large Mercedes limousine parked in front and he assumed it belonged to the German officers. He then entered the back door of the car and crouched himself down on the floor and waited. An hour later the two German officers came out of the Inn in a happy mood and, after drinking several bottles of the local wines they were laughing over their attempt to bed the Inn owner's daughter.

The Germans started the motor and drove to the main road. They stopped momentarily for traffic, just long enough for Bismarck to go into action. He shot them both in the back of the head. He then drove the auto to a secluded spot. He dragged them out of the auto and dumped them behind a bolder. He looked down at one of the officers and then a fascinating thought came to him. If he portrayed himself as a German officer he may be able to Con his way back to England. Driving the German car as an Italian peasant would be a dead givaway. He quickly removed the higher ranking officer's clothes and put them on. He placed his own clothes under the back seat of the Limo, he may need them later. Bismarck removed whatever cash and identification they had on them and concealed their bodies with branches and leaves. There was a brief case on the front seat containing the officers orders and Italian money. When he was sure the coast was clear he drove the vehicle back to the Inn. Bismarck then sat down in the restaurant and ordered himself a fine chicken dinner. He will pay for the dinner with his newly acquired Italian denaro in Lira.

After dinner he was feeling a little tired and was still not fully recovered from the crash. It was only 4:00 P.M. and still daylight so he paid for a room at the Inn and immediately fell asleep with his German clothes on. He woke up the next morning at 5:00 A.M., cleaned up and went back down to the restaurant. He wasn't thinking clearly and as he walked into the restaurant two German officers stood up and saluted him sharply. Bismarck was not sure what rank he had but he obviously outranked them. He saluted back and took a seat at the far end of the restaurant.

As he was having his breakfast one of the officers came over to him and asked him in German what was his destination. Bismarck was afraid to answer for fear of being detected but he had to chance it. Meanwhile, he had his hand on his pistol just in case. He simply told the officer in his best German that he was headed for Milan. The officer said that they were headed for Rome and asked if he needed a lift. Bismarck told them he didn't and the officer went back to his table. He was a little concerned that the officer may have detected him, but when he overheard one officer tell the other one that he is Bavarian he knew he was safe. His accent was good enough to fool them, he thought.

The officers finally left but were standing outside the Inn each having a cigarette. They were obviously waiting for him.

When Bismarck walked out one of the officers apologized and asked to see his identification. Bismarck produced a folder with the dead German's credentials. The one officer examined them and showed them to his partner.

He heard the other officer say, "This is not von Bourn, I know him personally."

The first officer's hand moved toward his gun and quick as lightning Bismarck drew his own and shot them both dead. He then ran to the Limo and took off. He surmised that the officers didn't detect his German accent as being false but that it just so happened that they knew the officer he was impersonating.

In the initial confusion Bismarck never had a chance to examine the papers of the dead officers. When he had the opportunity he stopped the vehicle and opened their folders. He looked at the picture of the dead officer he was impersonating and noted that his rank and name was Major William von Bourn who has been assigned as head of communications over the German occupational headquarters in Rome. Bismarck did not resemble the German's picture at all. The dead officer had light hair, probably blond, while his own was brown. If he was going to impersonate this von Bourn he will have to replace the picture with one of his own. Meanwhile, he cut out the present picture just in case he was stopped again and could claim it was destroyed. He threw the other dead officers papers in the bushes.

Bismarck drove into Milan and found a small Italian hotel. He registered his name as von Bourn and was escorted to his room by a bell hop. He wasn't sure if he still wanted to play the part of a German officer so the first thing he did was change his clothes back into his civilian ones and later left the hotel to see if he could contact the Italian underground. He wandered through the streets and did some shopping. He decided that his clothes were too British looking so he purchase more suitable local attire. His Italian may be good enough to fool the Germans but was not good enough to fool the Italians. He had to be careful.

Bismarck was well aware of the underground guerrilla movement against Mussolini and somehow he had to make contact with them. He had heard from other pilots that they have helped many downed pilots escape back to England. He purchased a newspaper and began reading it and on the second page he noticed a list of local Italian soldiers that were killed in the war. He glanced through some of the names and one particular name struck his attention.

It said, "General Milito was killed in Africa by British cannon fire. He is survived by his wife Countessa Lisa and their daughter Maria."

He thought for a moment, "Could it be my Lisa?"

He had to find out and was getting very apprehensive. He hailed a cab and asked the driver if he happened to know if this countessa Lisa in the paper was in Milan.

"Si. She lives in a mansion on a hill top overlooking Milano."

"Take me there at once."

The cab was a pretty old auto and it was struggling to make that climb. The driver had to stop periodically to cool the engine and add water. Bismarck was becoming impatient and had to endure this eternal waiting. It took approximately two hours to drive just twenty miles but they finally made it. Bismarck asked the driver to wait for a moment.

As he stepped out of the cab he looked up at the mansion. It was very old and needed paint and repair. The grounds were bare from neglect. He could picture how it looked before the war when the Count was alive and ruling over his serfs. He felt a little compassion for Lisa but he hasn't seen her yet.

He knocked on the front door and a woman dressed in black answered. He looked at her and for the moment they were both startled.

She then said, "William?"

He answered, "Yes. It's me."

"Oh, my gosh. What are you doing in Italy, especially with this dreadful war going on?"

"May I come in? I will tell you all about it."

She said yes. Bismarck went back to the cab, paid the cab driver and went inside. The driver sat in the cab for a moment contemplating what he had just witnessed. He was becoming suspicious of this situation. He had detected her unusual reaction when she first saw this stranger. He was pretty sure that this man was a foreigner from his pathetic spoken Italian, and maybe he's a spy. He may want to inform the proper authorities, but first he will try to extract money from this wealthy countessa to keep his mouth shut. He will wait for the opportune moment.

The first thing Bismarck tried to do was to put his arms around her, but she held him away. "Sorry, William, but I have just become a widow. Please be patient. Italians don't like to see their widows make friends with another male so soon after their husbands death. You understand."

Lisa would have loved to feel his strong arms around her but there were servants in the house. They would resent it. She did fall in love with Bismarck back in the states but when she never heard from him she reluctantly married General Milito who had been courting her for years. Her father kept coaxing her into this marriage because his own health was failing. The General would provide her with a secure and proper life she deserves after he's gone. General Milito came from an aristocratic and wealthy family.

The night before Lisa returned to Italy from Malibu she had confessed everything to Bismarck. She told him what her real name was and that there was a conspiracy against him that was instigated by Mr. Nichols. A counter sting was planned to destroy him financially, but some of the men, especially Pietro Columbo, wanted him killed.

At that time in Malibu, Bismarck confessed to her that he also had fallen in love with her and told her to go back to Italy where she would be safe. He will take care of things in America and when the controversy is over he will come to Italy to marry her. The problem was that he was on the run from the mob and knew the Italian Mafia would be watching Lisa's home. He didn't want to implicate her so he never wrote to her for fear of her life. They would probably even read her mail.

Now that she saw him again she knew that she was still madly in love with him. They went into the study and Lisa poured him a glass of red wine. "Why didn't you at least write to me?" Lisa asked.

"I couldn't my love. The mob was after me and I was afraid they might harm you. Even today, the Mafiosos are still after me.

Then when I heard you were married I assumed that you no longer loved me. I gave up all hope of ever seeing you again."

"*Mio cuoro.* I never stopped loving you."

When she said this Bismarck became very uncomfortable. He wanted to hold her and kiss her but for the moment he cannot even touch her. It was frustrating for him. She was as beautiful as ever even though she was dressed in dreary black mourning attire. It was a custom he understood but didn't agree with.

Just then a little girl came running into the room and Lisa introduced her to Bismarck in Italian. "Mr. Jones, I would like you to meet my daughter, Maria. Maria this is Signore Jones." She avoided telling her that he came from America.

"Please to meet you, Signore Jones."

"And I you. How old are you, Maria?"

"I'm eight years old."

Bismarck was surprised at her age. It didn't seem that long since the last time he had made love with Lisa at the Malibu beach house. Bismarck smiled at the little girl. He could see she was the spitting image of her mother.

"She's beautiful, Lisa. She look's just like you."

"She's spoiled rotten, just as I was, but I adore her."

"Mama, can I go outside and play? There doesn't seem to be any bombing today."

"Yes, my love. But as soon as you hear the sirens I expect you to come right home and down into the basement with me."

"Yes, Mama. I will." She left them both standing together adoring her as she departed.

"Now William, tell me how did you get here."

Bismarck related his escape to her and all about his being in the Canadian Air Corps. He told her that the mob was still after him. He explained how he was shot down over Munich and how he landed in Lake Como. Bismarck told her how he got to Milan by impersonating a German Major who was being transferred to Rome as their communications commander.

"My German is better than my Italian and I could easily pass myself off as a Bavarian."

His impersonation of a German officer caused Lisa to ponder a thought. She began pacing the room thinking to herself and not saying a word. She finally picked up a phone and made a call.

"I'm having a friend over to meet you, William. Maybe he can help you escape back to England."

While they waited they began reminiscing about the past. Bismarck repeated that he was still madly in love with her and if this war ever ended he would definitely marry her. She said she still feels the same way about him but they would have to wait the proper mourning period of at least a year. There was a knock at the front door and this time the maid answered it. A man came into the room looking more like a peasant farmer.

When the maid left she introduced him to Bismarck. "Mario, I want you to meet Signore Jones. He's a Canadian pilot and was shot down by the Germans."

At that moment Bismarck pulled out his gun. He didn't expect Lisa would turn him in. "Wait, William. You don't understand. Mario is a member of the underground partisans who are dedicated to fight against Mussolini and Hitler. His cause is to ally the partisans with the Americans and the British and help them win this war. Don't you see, I'm also a member. Mussolini calls us traitors but we say he is, for involving our country in a war with Hitler."

Bismarck was a little ambivalent but then he could detect that she was sincere and reholstered his gun in the back of his trousers.

She continued, "We have been smuggling many pilots back to England. We are on your side and want to aid the allies into winning this dreadful war. Our people hate Mussolini for what he has done. I joined them before my husband was killed in this useless and unpopular war. I asked Mario to come here to help you, but first I want him to hear your story about your German impersonation."

Bismarck then repeated the story of him killing four Germans and how he was able to fool German soldiers that he was a German Major. The only problem he had was that the picture on his victim's identification papers did not match his own.

Mario then spoke, "This all sounds too good to be true, my friend. What a wonderful opportunity. Don't you understand?

What I am proposing is that you should continue to impersonate the German Major and act as a spy for us in Rome. Being in charge of the communications center will give you access to all of the German movements in Italy. Don't you see how valuable you will be to our cause."

"Wait a minute here. I'm no hero. I just happened to get into the fighting to avoid being assassinated. Your asking too much of me. Anyway, I don't think I could get away with it. No thank you."

On the side, Lisa told Mario to leave them and she would try to persuade him. Mario caught the message and left. After Lisa and Bismarck had their supper, they talked some more about the States. Lisa then showed him his room which happens to be just across the hall from hers. Later that evening Bismarck heard his door slowly being opened. He reach for his gun that was stashed under his pillow. When the intruder came close Bismarck quickly jumped up to defend himself, but then he saw who it was.

"Lisa. What are you doing here?"

"Shush, my love," and she crawled into his bed.

They began making passionate love together and Bismarck went wild. It's been a long time since he had a woman, but now he is making love to his sweetheart, his only true love. They finally reach the ultimate apex of their performance and climaxed together. She stayed with him throughout the night and made love with him several more times.

When he awoke the next morning she was gone, but moments later the door opened and there she was carrying a tray of food. This time she was not in black but in a pink night gown. She placed the tray over his legs in bed and sat on the edge, admiring him. He looked into her beautiful blue eyes and knew he was a goner. He was still madly in love and nothing, not even this war, is going to stop him from being with her forever.

She broke the silence first, "Are you happy, my love?"

"Yes I am, Lisa. This is truly the first time that I am contemplating settling down and raising a family. If it weren't for this damned war... Why don't we get married, anyway?"

"Sounds like a good idea, but how can you stay here and be

my husband. You will eventually be detected as an enemy and be taken away to a prison camp for the duration of the war. I couldn't stand to be away from you that long, William." She was careful not to suggest anything.

Bismarck began thinking to himself. "Maybe I could get away with being a German officer and we could go to Rome as husband and wife. That would even help my cover better being married to an Italian countess. You know I think it would work, and we would be together always."

"I agree, *mio amore.* I think it's a wonderful idea."

"But what about your mourning period."

"To hell with my mourning period. I have waited too long for this moment and I'm not going to let anything get in the way of our happiness."

The Impersonator

Several days later, when Bismarck was driven back to town by Lisa's handyman, he noticed that the German limo was still where he had parked it, in front of the hotel. He cautiously went into the hotel and walked up to his room slowly. His door was still locked. He then entered and looked around the room carefully to make sure it hadn't been searched. He was satisfied it wasn't and decided to lay down for a nap before he began executing the plan.

The plan that Mario, Lisa, and Bismarck agreed to was that he should continue to impersonate the German Major in Rome. First, he will go back to Lisa's home dressed as the German officer and there they will be married in a local church to be witnessed by a small party of Italians and possibly a German soldier who is usually stationed by the church. Unfortunately, he will have to use the German's name he acquired for the marriage ceremony, but when the war is over they plan to remarry using his own name.

Before the marriage ceremony took place, Mario had Bismarck's picture taken with his German uniform on and had it professionally placed on his identification folder so that he will have less trouble passing himself off as Major William von Bourn. Also, the fact that his real name is William may be an asset incase he was challenged by someone calling out his first name to see if he was an impostor.

Lisa later mentioned to Bismarck that she had a bad encounter with the taxi cab driver who had first brought him to her Villa. "He wanted to blackmail me or he would reveal to the authorities that you are an American spy. Mario and his men quickly disposed of him so we are sure that you are in the clear. That was a close call."

Bismarck wasn't completely satisfied with this latest discovery. What if the cab driver told it to someone else, he thought? He didn't like any loose ends in any caper but he kept it to himself. He was already not sure he wanted to go through with this caper. But when he looked into Lisa lovely eyes he said to himself, "What's the use."

Bismarck was now sitting in the living room with Lisa and was thinking about something that she had mentioned back in Malibu, California. "Lisa, before we made love the first time in Malibu you mentioned that you had a horrible experience with a man. Don't you think, before we get married, that you should tell me about it? I prefer not to find out about a bad situation in our lives indirectly after we are married."

"Very well, William. I agree. I don't want to start this marrage off on the wrong foot. When I was fourteen I was already in full blossom. I could easily pass for eighteen years of age because of my height and my bust size. There was a distant cousin who used to come to visit us occasionally from Venice. His name is Count Marco Del Monte. When I was very young he would always play with me. Sometimes he would put me to bed and tell me stories but he would always touch me in the wrong places. I didn't understand at the time that he was a deviate. When I turned fourteen he did more to me than just touch me. The first time it happened he was visiting with my parents. They had to go to the king's ball so he volunteered to stay and watch over me. After I had gone to bed that night he came into my room and raped me. He then threatened me and said that if I mentioned this to anyone he would kill me and my parents. He would later visit us whenever my father went out of town for business and would rape me again.

This went on periodically for the next year until one day my father came back too soon and caught him with me in bed. There was a struggle and my father, who always carries a gun for protection, shot him. We thought he was dead but somehow he survived.

My dad did not press charges because Del Monte was very powerful in the Fascist party and was close friends with Mussolini. He's alive and living in Venice. Now that my father is dead he still tries to see me whenever my husband is away at war. I wrote to him that if he ever came near me again my guards would kill him. This has not stopped him, nonetheless, because he still tries to call me and writes me despicable letters. I don't know what to do about him. When he finds out my husband is dead I'm sure he will be more aggressive. So now, if you don't approve of what had happened to me and don't want to marry me, I will understand."

"Don't be silly. I love you. It doesn't make any difference to me and don't you worry about you cousin any longer. After we are married I'm sure he won't bother you again." While Bismarck was listening to her story he was having a hard time containing his temper. He will inevitable deal with this Count Del Monte at an appropriate time. He will have his own vendetta.

The marriage was meant to be a quiet family affair but the local peasants became aware of it and were upset about her being married so soon after her husband's death and especially to a German officer. Her first husband was considered a war hero who was killed in action fighting for Italia.

"*Disgrazia,*" they yelled at the couple as they left the church, and instead of throwing the traditional rice of farewell at them they began throwing rotten tomatoes.

Bismarck covered Lisa with his coat as he helped her climb into his German limo. One tomato hit him square in the face and when he entered the car on the driver side Lisa coudn't help herself and laughed. He was not amused, however. She began wiping his face with a towel while still giggling. He then started the motor and headed for Rome. On the way he continuely complained to Lisa about the way they were treated and said those people should be taught a lesson. She simply ignored him and eventually he stopped.

That night they stayed in a small hotel at the outskirts of the ancient city. Many Italians despised the "*Tedescos*" (Germans) because they felt that it was Hitler who had forced their country into this stupid war. When some of the guests in the Italian hotel saw the German Major come into the lobby with the once popular and beautiful Countessa from Milan they were bitter, and began making indecent remarks and called her a "*puttana*" (whore) and sneered at her. Bismarck saw a few German soldiers in the lobby and gave them a command to stop this disorder. The soldiers immediately pushed the Italians around and slapped one of the leaders across his face. Bismarck then yelled out to the manager in his poor Italian that he expects no more disturbances while he is here or he will close the place down. The frightened manager promised that it will never happen again.

When they went upstairs and were finally settled in, Lisa came close to Bismarck and whispered, "Mr. Jones, you astonish me. You were certainly magnificent acting the part of a German officer. You were wonderful, but will you be that forceful in bed?"

With that que Bismarck grabbed her and wrestled her onto the bed. She began giggling and then began laughing as she was acting defiantly. They finally bonded their relationship with passionate love. They were truly in love with each other.

The next morning Bismarck drove to the German headquarters in Rome. This will be his initial test to pass himself off as a German officer. He stopped in front of the headquarter's entrance and immediately instructed the guards in his Bervarian German accent to have his auto washed and cleaned. He attempted to give the impression that he was a demanding commander. He then went into a converted mansion, walking noisily on the marble floor with the heels of his black leather boots. He approached the information desk very smartly and demanded that all officers are to report to his office immediately. He showed the desk clerk his credentials and his orders that came directly from General Decker, the commanding officer in Berlin. The desk clerk quickly ushered him upstairs to the second floor to a large bedroom that was converted to an office especially for him.

"We were expecting you a few days ago, sir. And where is your assistant, Lieutenant Gruber?" asked the clerk.

"We were attacked by a British fighter who was strafing the area with machine gun fire. My assistant was killed but I survived by jumping over a stone wall. Gruber didn't have a chance."

A half hour later ten officers entered the room. Bismarck introduced himself and asked each officer to provide his name, his rank, and his duties at the headquarters. After this was done he dismissed all of the officers except his next highest ranking member, Captain Max Dryer.

"Captain Dryer. I understand you were the first officer to acquire this mansion from an Italian nobleman for military purposes. At least that's what it say's here in my orders."

"Yes. It's true, sir. The nobleman was reluctant to give up his estate so we unfortunately had to dispose of him. He was no great loss, Herr Commandant," replied Dryer.

Bismarck tried to hide his temper over this unnecessary killing and said, "Good. Since I'm new here I want you to give me a tour of the facilities and update me on all of our activities. I have a job to do and the sooner I get started the better." He certainly looked and acted the part well.

Captain Dryer was quite familiar with these temporary new officers that were assigned to this detail. He assumed the Major was probably appointed by some general who was friends of the Major's family. He's seen it happen before. So far, in the two years that he has been here, five commanders paraded through. He will humor this one just like he did the others. They all knew absolutely nothing about communications and instead of relying on Dryer's judgement they would make fools of themselves by initiating poor decisions. Dryer felt that Bismarck will last about six months and then he would be transferred out, he thought.

Captain Dryer was a man in his late thirties. He was tall and muscular but was not particularly good looking. His face had a scar on his right cheek along the chin line. He had jet black hair that was cut very short. He never was promoted above captain because of his limited education. He was an electronic technician prior to the war working for a Berlin radio station. Because of his age and his experience in radio repair he was made an officer and his first assignment was to set up this communications center in Rome. After that assignment was completed he was promoted to the rank of captain.

"Before we begin, Captain, I want to inform you that I was just married today to an Italian Countess from Milan. After our tour of the facilities is over I want you to arrange suitable quarters for me and my bride. In a day or so, I will be taking a couple of weeks vacation with her on the Italian Riviera, so I expect you to handle all the necessary details here and run things while I'm away."

"Yes, Commandant."

Now the captain was sure he won't last long. Marriage to an Italian during this war was frowned upon by the high command, and then taken an unapproved vacation on top of it all was unheard of. Doesn't he know there is a war going on? When they hear about it back in Berlin, he'll be relieved of his command in short order. Dryer himself has an Italian mistress whom he adores. He was tempted to marry her also, but he knows the rules. He certainly didn't want to be transferred back to Germany for insubordination because it meant fighting on the Russian front.

Their vacation on the Italian Riviera completely solidified their marriage. Bismarck and Lisa spent days in their hotel room together making love and only left their bed to ordered food. Bismarck couldn't believe how much he loved Lisa. He never experienced this much desire for any one woman before. Even his love for Cathy Sullivan was not as profound. There was no doubt about it, Bismarck was truly in love. He could never be the same again. When this war is over he promised himself that he will live a normal life and have a fine family. No more Con games, he said to himself. Extortion and larceny will be hard for him to give up because he's been at it too long. He purposely left out gambling in his vow.

After Bismarck and Lisa returned back to Rome from his delayed honeymoon, Headquarters was receiving numerous coded messages on radio from Berlin. It was obvious to the German commanders in Berlin that an invasion from Africa by the Allies would occur somewhere in southern Italy. Exactly where was still unknown. One important message that was directed to Major von Bourn was to establish a series of new communication stations in southern Italy, especially in Sicily.

Bismarck acted quickly. "Captain Dryer. I'm given you orders to open up communication stations at key locations in Italy as directed by our high command. Take as many men as you need. If the Allies attack they will come from Africa to Sicily or Calabria, so those two areas are the first places you shall install your transmitters and radios. You will be in charge of those two facilities. When you have completed your mission I want all communications to come through this headquarters in code. Then I will personally relay only the important messages to Berlin, understood?"

"Yes, Herr Commandant."

"Good. We don't need to overload our communications network to Berlin with a lot of gibberish, so this center will screen all messages. When can you start, Captain?"

The Captain then snapped to attention by clicking his heels. "Herr Commandant. Before I begin, I have a request to make of you. You see, sir. I am seeing an Italian lady myself and I would like your permission to take her with me?"

"Ah... So I am not the only one who has fallen for these lovely Italian girls. I understand your predicament fully, Captain. You have my permission, of course, but only after you have established the new stations in Sicily and Calabria. I'm sure you will work extra hard to speed up this project so that you will be able to send for your sweetheart as soon as possible."

"It will be done in record time. Thank you, sir."

The Escape

Over the next year Bismarck had a sweet set up. He was living high on the hog and the Italians were now treating him royally. He assumed that the underground had passed the word to cooperate because, all of a sudden, the Italians were no longer calling his wife a whore. Even the Italian servants at the hotel that they were staying at were paying them their utmost respect and acted much more pleasantly. Lisa was quite pleased. Now they were very happy together. If it could only last forever, but war is war.

Bismarck was doing his counter spying well. As the messages came in from Southern Italy he would modify them slightly. One major message that came through said, "It is estimated that an invasion was expected to take place in Southern Sicily." The message was simply modified to say Southern Calabria instead. It was only an estimate, anyway, so no one at the command post in Berlin was deeply excited or even questioned the message.

This went on for the better part of a year when finally Bismarck received a message from Sicily on October 23, 1942. It said, "Army Lt. Gen. Bernard L. (Monty) Montgomery, has ordered 1,000 array guns to open fire on the German-Italian front line in Egypt. This will be the start of the Allied counter-offensives that would roll back the German conquests in Africa."

The message that was sent back to Berlin from the Rome headquarters simply said that the Germans and Italians are holding back a fierce barrage of cannon fire from the British, and no more. Most of the time Bismarck would only transmit half the message, this way if he was investigated they couldn't accuse him of being completely wrong since he could claim that some of the message was lost in transmission.

Then on Nov. 4, the allies launched the greatest amphibious assault ever seen at that time. Some 84,000 American and 23,000 British troops landed in Morocco and Algeria and captured those territories. The message that was sent to Berlin stated, "There was an attack on Morocco and Algeria but there was no further information to report."

One day Bismarck spotted a Gestapo agent snooping around the building. He was dressed in civilian clothing and no one stopped him. Bismarck was now getting worried. He immediately went home and told Lisa that the jig is up and that she had better get ready to shove off.

"But how do you know that he's wise. It might be just a routine visit. We can't leave just like that. You must find out for sure what he wants, William. I'm so happy now, we must be sure."

"Lisa. I have always had an instinct about trouble and when to get out of a con job. It hasn't let me down yet. I know we are being investigated. Don't you understand, if we are captured they have ways of making us talk and it would only be a matter of time when all of your underground friends will be implicated. We may even be executed. We must leave now!"

"Very well. I will miss this place. Everything was going so well. Anyway, I must tell you one other problem we are having. I hope it won't disturb you but I'm expecting a child."

"Oh no. Not now. Jesus Christ. How far are you?"

"Two months."

"Well, that gives us some time. Shit!"

"Don't you want this baby? I could have an illegal abortion."

"Hell no. I don't want you going to no damn butcher. I want that child, do you understand? It's just that, I wasn't ready for it, that's all. I'm sorry for the outburst."

"Very well then, I will get in touch with the underground and see how they can help us," answered Lisa.

Lisa picked up the phone and made a few calls. Bismarck called headquarters and told his secretary that he was not feeling very well and that he will take a few days off. He wanted to delay the Gestapo's questions to give them a head start in their escape.

Bismarck changed into his Italian clothing once again and Lisa dress up as an average peasant. They carried as little as possible. They waited near the front door of the hotel and were eventually picked up by an Italian partisan driver who drove them to a small home outside of Rome. There they were greeted by a tall Italian man who had a belt of ammunition slung over his shoulder and across his body. He was carrying a rifle and he also had a 45 caliber pistol in a holster at his side. He was fairly attractive but rugged looking with his week old beard. He was smiling when he greeted them.

"*Buongiorno,* Countessa and Colonel Perkins. Please come into my headquarters so that we can discuss your escape. I'm referred here as Romano. My real name is of no significance."

His real name was Georgio Francini who was related to Mussolini's wife. He didn't want to incriminate his cousin over his association against the dictator so he took the name Romano. He was an accomplished partisan fighter who had destroyed numerous German and Italian convoys. Romano was wanted by Mussolini's personal leather black guards whose orders were to kill him on sight. Romano was in control of several hundred partisan men and women who played havoc on the Germans.

The house they were in was more of a hut which was originally used by peasant working on the farm. It was a good cover for the partisan underground movement. When they entered the home, Romano asked them to sit at a very large solid oak table centered in the middle of the room. The table could seat ten people and Bismarck could see that it was extensively used by the visible burnt cigarette marks and wine stains as a result of many drinking sessions. These partisan men were killers and would fight to the end against the Fascist government and Germans. Their main objective was to delay or destroy any movement of military goods by the Germans to Southern Italy. This meant blowing up rail lines, trains and bombing truck caravans. No German prisoners were ever taken alive during these raids. There were many partisan movements all over Italy. Romano covered only the Roman area.

The partisans were a major defiance against the German high command. There was the story of a famous Italian, Vice Brigadier Salvo D'Acquisto, (Courtesy of Rudy D'Angelo) who sacrificed his life to save 21 of his countrymen from execution. Salvo was born in Naples on October 15, 1920 and was promoted to Vice Brigadier in the Royal *Carabinieri,* Italy's military police force in 1942.

On December, 1942, D'Acquisto was sent to the village of Torrimpietra, 30 kilometers north of Rome. In 1943, Field Marshal Kesselring, commander of German forces in Italy, issued orders to all concerned that every act of violence commited by partisans must be punished immediately. If any German soldier is killed by them several Italian males will be arrested and executed. Should the troops be fired at from a village, the village will be burnt down.

On September 22, 1943, two German paratroopers were killed by partisans in the village of Torrimpietra. When the troopers got drunk and wreaked havoc in the village they killed several civialians. The partisans took revenge. The German NCO in charge gave the order to take 10 Italian hostages for each dead German. They will be executed unless the partisans that commited the murders come foward and confess. D'Acquisto pleaded with the Germans that these people are innocent of murder, to no avail. Instead, D'Acquisto was also taken as a hostage along with another innocent man who happened to ride by on a bicycle.

The next morning, 22 hostages were taken to an open field where they were ordered to dig their own graves. D'Acquisto then made a brave move. He told the commander that he alone was reponsible for the killing of the two Germans. He said that he was dressed as a civilian when he threw a hand grenade into the taveran and the explosion killed the two paratroopers. The commander didn't believe him but in order to fulfill the Field Marshal's directive of retaliation he shot D'Acquisto in the chest. He then fired a final shot into his head. He turned to his own men and gave the orders to free the remaining 21 hostages. The commander's report to the Field Marshal was excepted with no questions.

Salvo D'Acquisto became a national hero and was bestowed Italy's equivalent of the Medal of Honor. This true tale was one of many atrocities that went on under the German command of Italy and why Italians despised the *Tedescos.*

As Bismack and Lisa sat down at the partisan's table one of

Romano's men poured a glass of Chianti wine for each of them. Romano raised his glass and said, "*Salute tuta* and to our cause. May the allies destroy all the *Tedescos* who have been destroying our country."

Romano then sat down and spread out an old map of Europe on the table. It was frayed very badly from extensive use but still discernable.

"With you permission, Colonel, I will show you the different routes that you may wish to take back to England. They are all very dangerous. First, you could go to Africa by way of Sicily. The Allies are still fighting there and you may run the risk of being captured by the Germans. In another month or so this might be the best way to go, as the British and Americans are slowly capturing more and more territories in North Africa. Today, however, I think the safest route to take is through Spain to Portugal. We can provide you with a fishing motor-boat that you can take to Genoa, but you will have to steer it yourselves. To go directly to Spain across the Ligurian Sea would be disastrous. Germans patrol boats are sinking any and all boats without warning that they encounter three miles off shore. So you must hug the shore line as a fishing boat.

"When you reach Genoa, land your boat in slip near a restaurant called Mama Lucia's. The slip will have a red and white flag at the end of the pier. There you will contact a Signore Giuseppe Maggio who can be located by the bartender in that same restaurant. You will use the pass-word *Castano* (horse chestnut) to the bartender. After you meet Maggio, he will instruct you on the rest of your journey from there. Is this a satisfactory arragement for both of you?"

"Yes. We understand. Will you provide us with guns just in case?" asked Bismarck.

"If you wish, but I think you will have a better chance if you were unarmed. But that is up to you."

Bismarck decided he wanted gun protection so Romano agreed to provide him with a German machine gun that he had confiscated in a previous raid and had it mounted on board. He also gave each of them a pistol. Romano then commanded his men to put freshly caught fish in a hold at the back of the boat so if they are stopped by the Germans they could pass themselves off as fishermen by displaying a resent catch.

Now that there escape was agreed upon Ramano ordered dinner. They were served a meal of pasta and fried fish. Romano and some of his men began singing Italian folk songs and were drinking wine heavily. They finally fell asleep on the floor or wherever they could find an empty spot. Lisa and Bismarck were given the main bed in a separate room.

While lying in bed Lisa was getting concerned. She said, "*Mio cuore.* Wouldn't it be better if you made this trip alone? I think you would have a better chance of making it by not having a pregnant woman tagging along."

"Nonsense. We will make it to Genoa together, my love. I'm a good sailor and I know these waters fairly well. After we get to France we will see how to travel to Portugal. Now rest my darling. We have a long trip ahead of us."

The next morning they both left by boat from the port city of Fiumicino and headed north. They decided it would be better to sail in the daylight right under the German's noses and pass themselves off as fishermen. At night they would most likely be stopped and boarded. It's over three hundred miles from Rome to Genoa and with their boat traveling at 10 knots, and with a little luck, Bismarck figured they could make it in three days. The machine gun was hidden from sight with a tarpaulin cover. It was located in a forward fishing hold but could easily be raised with a hand crank and ready for action in a short order.

The first eighty miles went along smoothly. As they came near the Island of Giglio a small German harbor patrol approached them. Bismarck told Lisa to get inside the cabin and that he will handle it. There were three Germans on board a captain and two sailors. As they came close one sailor jumped onto Bismarck's fishing boat and tied their boats together with a line. The German spoke poor Italian so Bismarck responded in broken German or tried to give the impression he was an Italian trying to speak German.

"Where's your catch," demanded the German sailor.

Bismarck pointed to the fish tank in the back of the boat but he sensed that this was more that just a search. Bismarck could always sense danger. He still had that instinct. The man acted peculiar, as though he was only interested in the catch and not about the crew. Normally, the first thing a German sailor would demand was to see their identifications papers or passports but this sailor didn't. Bismarck surmised that all they wanted was the fish which could be sold in town for some profit. Bismarck's gun was in a holster well hidden in the back of his pants. He was ready.

When the German saw the catch he was well pleased. "I see you had a fine day," he said with a cynical smile.

At that very moment the German went for his side arm but Bismarck pulled his own gun out much faster and shot the man dead. He then pushed him over the side. The two other Germans on the harbor boat heard the shot but assumed that their comrade had just killed the fisherman. It was their practice to kill the crew and tow the boat full of fish into port. It was a lucrative racket and these Germans were collecting a nice nest-egg for themselves while a war was goig on. They would also sell the fishing boat to a local Italian for a reasonable some. It was quite a business. War or no war there is always a racket going on, it seems.

Lisa was in the cabin at the time and didn't know what had happened as she heard the gun fire and just as she opened the cabin door Bismarck went into action. He quickly shot the other German sailor who was leaning on the rail of the German patrol, but the captain was still inside the pilot house trying to maintain the position of his own boat against Bismarck's boat and didn't notice his own man being shot. Bismarck quickly removed the Tarp and raised the machine gun from its position in the front hold. He began shooting at the German boat below the water line. The boat began taking on water. The captain, now realizing what had happened, panicked and abandoned the boat. He tried to swim towards the shore but Bismarck aimed his machine gun at him and blew his head off. He couldn't allow survivers to expose him. Bismarck quickly untied the German boat from his own boat and they both stood there and watched it sink slowly to the bottom.

"Why did you have to shoot them, William? They would

have let us go after they saw our catch."

"My dear. They weren't interested in us. They wanted the catch for themselves to sell on shore. If I didn't kill them first we would both be dead by now. I have to admit, though, it was a lucrative racket. These guys sure had some ingenuity. I have to respect them for that. You see Lisa, it takes one to know one."

Lisa couldn't believe Bismarck's remark. How could he praise these robbers after they just made an attempted to kill them both. She just doesn't understand that there is a certain bond between crooks who respect and appreciate the fine art of creative stealing. Bismarck would always recognize and admire any new ingenious approach in stealing. He also got a kick out of out-smarting them. He stood there for the longest time praising himself over this encounter. Lisa finally woke him up and said that they had better get going before another patrol boat came along.

The rest of the trip went smoothly and they had no trouble meeting Maggio who provided them with an auto. Bismarck was told to follow the coast into France and then onto Barcelona, Spain. He gave them French money and the name of a contact in Barcelona.

When they reached Monte Carlo, Bismarck couldn't help himself. He had to try his luck at the gambling tables. Lisa didn't mind him going because she wanted to go to a hotel and have a hot bath and sleep in a warm stable bed. She didn't sleep well on the boat that was constantly rocking back and forth with the waves.

The last time Bismarck was here he had to fight a dual with Karl Miller. He later had to kill his brother Hans in Malibu, California, who was attempting to have his revenge for Karl's death. This time he would be more careful. The first thing he did was convert his left over Italian Lira into French Franks to add to the Franks that Maggio gave him. With that money he bought himself a fine suit. After all, he couldn't go into a casino looking like a peasant.

When he was in the casino he first began to case the joint. He purposely walked in front of the dealers to make sure he was not recognized. He then sat down at the Baccarat table and began betting conservatively, but then he noticed that the dealer was favoring a pretty blonde girl with a German accent who was seated across the table from him. She always bet against the bank and the dealer's quick hands invariably pass her a nine count or close enough to win. The average player wouldn't be able to detect this maneuver but Bismarck was a pro and saw the dealer produce cards from his sleeve or the bottom of the deck. Bismarck simply grinned to himself and left the table.

He felt great, though. This was his kind of place. Gambling, crooked dealers and pretty girls. He sure missed the action. The fun of a set-up and then winning the game was the most thrilling sport for him. He wandered over to the roulette table and at first he watched the betting. Again he noticed that the dealer was manipulating the wheel by pressing his finger on a button on the side of the table. When the dealer twirled the wheel again Bismarck watched and waited and precisely at the right moment he place a stack of chips on red. He won the equivalent of five thousand dollars. It was child's play.

Another man across the table also had won big but when he looked up at Bismarck he acted peculiar. He quickly turned his head away acting conspicuously. Bismarck was aware of his maneuver but continued to play, anyway. It was easy to bet because all he had to do is follow the bets this stranger made. Bismarck picked him out as the dealer's accomplice after the first few bets were down. He thought there was nothing worse than a crooked dealer, but as long as he can get in on the scheme, why not make some easy money.

For no apparent reason, the man stopped betting and walked away from the table. Bismarck watched him carefully from the corner of his eye. The man walked up to a gentleman dressed in a formal tuxedo and began whispering something to him. Bismarck then knew he was detected. The last time he was in this casino he was almost arrested. He was allowed to leave but was not to enter this establishment again. This present situation is different. The man in the Tux looked more like a German Gestapo who was looking for spies, and Bismarck figured that the German was told that he was an American.

Bismarck left the table and began slowly working his way to

the front door. He looked at the reflection from a glass window of a store and noticed that the man in the Tux was following him. When he got to the lobby he quickly ran down a flight of marble stairs and out the front door. He went around a corner and waited. Sure enough the man in the Tux came bursting out looking both ways. The doorman pointed to his left. The man then ran in the direction where Bismarck was hiding. As he came close, Bismarck thrust a dagger into the man's heart and immediately ran from the scene. He entered the room where Lisa was bathing and told her that she will have to get dressed.

"I've been recognized. We have to get out of here fast."

"But William. I'm finally feeling clean again and now you say we have to go. William, please. I can't make it. I'm tired of running. I'm not leaving. Please go yourself. You will have a better chance, anyway."

"But my love, they may torture you."

"No they wont, my darling. I have friends here and they will hide me. Go, my darling. It's the only way."

Bismarck knew she was right but he was having second thoughts about leaving her again and this time she was carrying his child.

She again pleaded with him, "Go my love, please. I can take care of myself. When the war is over come back to me and we will have a proper wedding." By now her tears were visable. He had mixed emotions about leaving her again. He loved her so much he couldn't bear being without her.

He looked into her tearful eyes once more. He was still having second thoughts about leaving her alone. He knew she was right, however, and he could no longer delay his departure so he kissed her as she cried. Bismarck disappeared into the night but before he left he laid down on the bed half of his money with her.

Bismarck drove for hours through Southern France and finally reached the Spanish boarder. He was now playing the part of a Spanish businessman who was buying farm equipment in France. His Spanish was much better than his Italian and he could pass himself off as a native. At the boarder he presented his forged papers that Maggio gave him to the guard who carried the papers into an adjacent office. Bismarck was getting impatient so he removed a concealed weapon from under the seat and was ready to make a dash for it, if necessary. The guard finally came out and gave him back his passport and his other traveling papers. He was in the clear.

Even though General Franco claimed victory over the revolution in Spain the chaos in the east had not ended, and traveling was still difficult. He made it to the internal city of Zaragosa but ran out of petrol. In the city fuel was almost impossible to obtain. His French money was not acceptable in this interior region so he tried to exchange it in a local bank. He was refused. The teller saw his dilemma and gave him a folded note. When he was outside and read the note he noticed that the only thing written on it was an address. He went to that address and knocked on the door of a small stucco home. An old man answered. Bismarck gave him the note and the man let him in. They walked down a hall and into a back room. He entered the room and saw a old woman sitting in a couch. She said she would convert his money into Spanish rebel money for only half the French value. Bismarck was in no position to barter so he accepted the trade. The Spanish woman said that he can fill his tank out around the back of the house, for a price, of course. She would only accept Franks for payment since rebel money may not be worth the paper it's printed on.

Bismarcks ultimate goal was Lisbon, Portugal. From there it should be a piece of cake to get back to England. The problem was after he left the city of Zaragosa and was heading for Madrid his vehicle was stopped and confiscated by the rebels. He was then drafted into the rebel army, like it or not. All he could think of right now was, "Thank God I didn't take Lisa."

Even though Franco claimed victory many of the rebels did not surrender. They would fight to the end. Bismarck was given a rifle, ammunition and some heavy clothing. Winter was coming on and all he had with him was the suit that he bought in France. They allowed him to keep his own pistol. He was told to follow the rest of the rebels into the mountains and if he retreated he would be shot down in cold blood as a deserter.

The fighting was bitter. The dictator's troops were better

equipped but the rebels didn't quit. The fighting went on for months. If the rebels weren't dying from gun shot wounds they were dying from the cold or the lack of food. Bismarck was becoming desperate. When he came across a dead enemy soldier the first thing he did was exchange his shoes and dry socks. His patent leather shoes certainly did not protect him from the elements.

The fighting continued to be intense and when the rebels approached Madrid the commander gave the orders to his subordinates that there will be an all out effort to capture the city. Bismarck knew that this might be the end for the rebels to win back Spain so he had to make his escape the first chance he could. He and fifty other rebels were outside the city behind a wall that was being shelled by cannon bombs when all of a sudden there was a direct hit on the men thirty yards to his right. At least twenty men were either dead or wounded. The rest of the men close to him retreated in panic.

Bismarck remained and saw for the first time the chance he was waiting for. He removed his heavy rebel coat and threw away his rifle. He began working his way towards the enemy, hiding behind trees and homes that were destroyed. A military truck came by with a canvas back. Bismarck could see that no one was in the back so he ran and ran and finally jumped onto the back of the truck. He hid himself under a tarp and waited. As the truck moved out he could see that they were passing several of Franco's soldiers on foot who were heading for the front so he assumed the truck was going in the opposite direction towards the city of Madrid. After the truck reached the interior Bismarck jumped off the back and scampered behind a bombed-out auto.

Bismarck, by now, was freezing and hungry so he stood up and began walking nonchalantly and mingled with the peasants in the street. He noticed a young lady carrying a sack over her back walking away from the crowd and decided to follow her. She finally entered a small cottage that had its windows covered with blankets. All the glass windows in the cottage were shattered from the war bombs. Bismarck worked his way around the back of the cottage and climbed into a rear window of a bedroom. He crawled on the floor and peered though an open door. He saw that the woman had bread and flower in her sack which she placed on a table. There was a small boy at her side and a baby in a crib.

Bismarck decided to make his move. He removed his pistol and went into the room. The woman was startled and almost began screeming. He told the girl to be quiet or he would kill all of them.

"What do you want, Señor?"

"Food and clothing. I will not harm you if you do as I say."

"You do not need that gun, Señor. I will share our food with you. There is an overcoat in the closet in the bedroom. I will get it for you. You must be very cold because we have little heat to spare. Sit down, Señor. I have potato soup still hot in a kettle in the fire place."

She paid no attention to his gun and walked right passed him into the bedroom and returned with a heavy woolen coat. She could see that he was shivering. He immediately put the coat on and sat at the table. She laid a bowl of hot soup in front of him and without hesitation he began drinking the soup right out of the bowl. He reached for the bread and acted as though he was about to eat the whole loaf.

"Señor. Please. That is all the bread we have for all of us."

Bismarck then looked up and saw that they haven't eaten yet and he began to realize how low he had stooped.

"I'm sorry, Señora. It is very rude of me. Please, you and your son join me."

When they all sat down she asked him, "Señor, where did you come from? I can see by the suit you are wearing and from your accent that you are not from these parts."

Bismarck was now relaxed and began scrutinize her. He had a knack of knowing when he was in danger and from her reactions he figured he was fairly safe. Now that she had removed her shawl from over her head Bismarck could see she was rather attractive. He figured that she was in her early twenties and all alone because all the able body men were fighting the rebels or were rebels. He decided to take a chance on her.

"My name is William Perkins. I'm an American, but I am a

pilot in the Canadian Air Corps fighting for the British. I was shot down over Italy and I'm working my way to Lisbon. I will not harm you or your children as long as you don't try to turn me in."

"How interesting. Here we are fighting a revolution and you are fighting against the Nazis. In that case I will also tell you about myself. My name is Lolita Gonzales. As you can see I have two children. I am a widow. My husband was killed last year in the war against the rebels. Food is very scarce here but I managed to acquire some potatoes and bread through my parents and some friends. We are all suffering but somehow we manage to stay alive. Señor Perkins, you may stay as long as you wish. I will not inform the authorities about you. No one cares, anyway. We have all lost our loved ones and only want the fighting to stop."

"I thank you for your offer, Lolita, but I cannot stay long. I must find a way to get to Lisbon and back to England."

It began getting dark outside and the fireplace was ready to go out. There was only one bedroom in the cottage and she asked Bismarck if he didn't mind sleeping on the floor. She had enough blankets to cover all of them.

Bismarck was tired and he welcomed the opportunity to rest. He immediately fell asleep on the floor. This was the first time in months that he had slept under a roof and with a warm blanket. Fighting with the rebels was mostly outdoors in all kinds of foul weather. In the middle of the night Lolita got up from her bed and gazed through the door at Bismarck lying on the floor sound asleep. She said to herself, "He'll never make it to Lisbon alive, poor devil." She then went back to her bed.

The next morning she gave Bismarck her husbands clothes so that he wouldn't look too conspicuous in town with his expensive suit. He thanked her again for her hospitality and took off. On his way he came across a closed truck that was parked on the road side. He was wondering if he could steal it but all at once there was a massive explosion in front of him as the truck was blown up. Several local people ran up to the truck and began carrying items from it. Bismarck could only surmised that it was a supply truck loaded with food for the troops. He quickly went over to the truck, grabbed a large package of whatever and ran down the road. As he looked back he saw soldiers shooting at the peasants killing several of them. Bismarck ran around the corner and hid himself. When he saw the coast was clear and he wasn't being followed he headed back to Lolita's cottage. He knocked on her door and after she let him in he put the package on the table. She quickly began cutting away the sack with a knife and was surprised to see a beautiful ham butt preserved in salt. It was like a miracle.

"Where did you get this, Señor Perkins?" He related the story to her and could see how pleased she was.

She said, "This will last us several weeks if we ration ourselves."

Bismarck agreed and said, "The first thing we need is more fire wood. I'll be back," and he took off again.

He headed out but this time looking for wood or coal. The only wood available was from homes that were destroyed by cannons but they were stripped bare by the local peasants. He then saw a chained-linked fenced in a yard that had logs in it. A man was standing there with a rifle to protect the fire wood. Bismarck approached the man and offered to buy some wood with his rebel money. He was surprised when the man accepted it.

He said, "I don't know which side will win the revolution but I collect money from both sides to make sure I'm covered."

Bismarck grinned to himself. Here's a man playing the odds. It sure brings back memories. He brought back a handful of firewood to Lolita and made the trip several more times until there was enough wood to last them a couple of weeks. They celebrated that evening with a fine meal of roasted ham and potatoes. Lolita dressed up in her special Sunday clothes for the occasion and for the first time in years she began smiling. She was indeed a pretty girl with her long black hair now combed down over her shoulders. Bismarck wished he could do more for her but he knew that one day he had to leave. He decided to stay at least one more night.

That evening, as he was sleeping on the floor, he heard footsteps heading toward him. He had his gun ready just in case.

His blanket was raised and a naked body came close to him. It was Lolita cuddling up to him. Bismarck at first was reluctant to have an affair with her but then he figured that he may never see his beloved Lisa again. He was sure Lisa wouldn't mind one last fling. Bismarck didn't say anything, and began kissing her. They made love throughout the night. The only thing wrong with this situation was that it delayed his departure. He remained the rest of the week, but instead of sleeping on the floor he was now sleeping in her bed. When he was finally ready to leave he kissed her for the last time. He reached into his pocket and place a wad of rebel money on the table.

"You may be able to use this for awhile to help keep you and your children alive. I will always remember you Lolita. Some day I will pay you back for everything you did for me."

"You have already paid me back, Señor. I know I will never see you again but you will always remain in my heart."

"Goodby, Lolita. God bless you."

He was off again carrying some dried meat in a sack under his coat. He headed southwest on an old road for Lisbon which was still another 380 miles away.

When he hiked twenty miles south from Madrid he noticed that the fighting seemed to have subsided. The main fighting was to the east of the historic city. He was then able to hitch several rides freely without worrying about being picked up by Franco's army. When he reached the city of Merida he took a bus to Badajoz which is a boarder city between Spain and Portugal. He spent the night in Badajoz and the next morning he took another bus to Lisbon. After the bus arrived he immediately went to the English Embassy and was received by the British ambassador. The ambassador was very familiar with English pilots escaping from the Germans through Lisbon usually from Africa, but not through Spain. He didn't think it was at all possible with the rebels persisting on carrying on the revolution which, for all practical purposes, was over. He immediately scheduled Bismarck to fly back to England the next morning. Bismarck decided to use the time remaining that evening to explore the city of Lisbon.

He had heard of a special man in Lisbon called Espanosa.

Throughout the years as a Con artist Bismarck new that this man had exceptional talent in extortion and graft. Some considered him even a better Con artist than himself. He simply had to meet Espanosa before he left for England. After making a few inquiries he discovered there was a private gambling establishment located by the docks where Espanosa may be found. Through a cab driver he managed to uncover the Molta hotel that was running private gambling games. When he knocked on the door of the hotel the doorman refused to allow him entrance.

"Sorry, Señor. Only those with special invitations are allowed into this hotel." The doorman was armed and ready for any hostility.

Bismarck then wrote a note and handed it to the doorman. "Please give this note to Señor Espanosa. I'm sure he will let me come in."

Ten minutes later the doorman returned and asked Bismarck to enter. He was frisked and his gun was removed from the back of his trouser. Bismarck didn't stop him. "Please follow me, Señor." They walked down a hall to a large office. There he saw a man seated behind a desk who carefully examined Bismarck. He had seen Bismarck before while gambling at a Monte Carlo casino but wanted to make sure. He was still a little cautious but when he looked into Bismarcks eyes he was positive it was him. Again, his blue eyes were as good as a finger print. No one had colored eyes like his.

"So. You claim to be Bismarck Jones the great American confidence man and gambler. If you are the great Bismarck, you have quite a reputation even here in Portugal."

"Yes, I am Bismarck Jones. I have never been in Lisbon but I am looking foward to do doing business here." Bismarck was still wondering if he had to prove who he was.

"And what can I do for you, Mr. Jones?" He then knew that he was accepted. They talked for hours about a new scheme that Bismarck had concocted while he was in Italy. At about midnight Bismarck left for his own hotel and the next morning he was flown back to England.

At this point in the war, on September 8, 1943, King Victor

Emmanuel III and the government of General Pietro Badoglio surrendered the Royal Italian Army to the Allies. Mussolini was arrested and imprisoned. This pleased Bismarck who now knew that his wife, Lisa, would be safe from Mussolini's black leather guards. When the German war is finally over he will go back to her. But then there was a turn of event. Mussolini was later released by Hitler and made a puppet ruler of Italy. Italy was again under dictator control and Bismarck was not so sure of his wife's safety.

Back in England

When Bismarck reported back to the Canadian Air Corps headquarters in England he discovered so many things had changed while he was away. General Burchard had been killed during a German air raid over London. Most of the Canadian pilots that Bismarck knew were either killed or wounded and were sent back to Canada. There was a new Colonel Jefferies in charge. As Bismarck walked through the door of his old office the new colonel, who was standing along side his old desk, promptly saluted him. Bismarck saluted back but he didn't know why since they are both of the same rank.

"When I heard that you made it back safely, General, I was elated. You're a hero. We learned all about your experiences in Europe especially about the spying you did in the communications center in Rome, Italy. It was a great feat and Canada is proud of you."

"Wait a minute," said the bewilder Biamarck. Why did you call me, General?"

"Oh. You don't know? Sir, you have been promoted to General and your orders are to take over the duties of the late General Burchard. Your official promotion is on your desk. We heard that you had escaped but, for a long time, we didn't know where you were. Then we received a wireless from the English Embassy in Lisbon that informed us that you were still alive. Welcome aboard to your new command, sir."

Bismarck just sat down in his office chair dumbfounded. He thought to himself, "My gosh. What's going on? All I wanted was a cushy job and now I'm considered a hero and, to top it off, they made me a General." He excused the colonel and began stairing into space. Then he thought about the Palace. He decided to call Mary who was still running the Palace.

"Mary. This is Bill. How are you?"

"Bill. Is that you? When did you get back? Harry and I thought you were dead." She was completely genuine in her surprise.

"No, as you can tell I'm fine. How's business?"

"Just fine, Bill. The money is still rolling in. By the way, before you hear it from someone else, Harry and I are married."

"I'll be," was all he could say.

"I hope you are not mad at us? It was more of a matter of convenience. It made it easier to do business."

"Of course I'm not not mad. Why should I be? Congratulations. I'll be around tomorrow and we can talk and catch up on business. See you."

Harry Stark didn't waste any time. Bismarck knew he was ambitious and he would take advantage of any situation to get ahead. He's as crooked as they come, but he was perfect in the position he had been assigned to. He assumed Harry married her when he thought that Bismarck was dead and he could take over the business. After all, the business is illegal anyway and there were no contracts written. The only establishments that Bismarck legally owned were the Palace and the two warehouses. Bismarck figured that he had better watch out for Harry Stark. He's not to be trusted.

The next morning he went to the Palace and was greeted with open arms by both Mary and Harry. The place still looked the same. The casino was empty for the moment but later that evening it will be jumping with soldiers and sailors. Bismarck motioned to Harry to follow him and they both entered his old office. Inside Bismarck could see signs that Harry had already taken over. He sat behind his desk and asked Harry to pour him a drink.

"Well Harry, how's business?"

"Great, boss. We have one major problem though. The Americans want to confiscate the ships we've been using. They are investigating us and want to close us down. They also see the advantage of using our very fast ocean liners as cargo ships to suppliment their slow moving Liberty cargo ships." He acted all business like.

"How is our storage situation?" questioned Bismarck.

"We are full to the brink again. Our next and last shipment is due any day now."

"Okay. Let the Americans have the ships. We couldn't stop them anyway since I am not the registered owner. We could live very comfortably with the sales we receive from the warehouse and the income from the Palace. The war cannot last much longer so we will have to end all of our activities here in England. The Allies have taken over Africa and I'm sure they will soon be mounting a major attack on Sicily. At least that's the information I received while I was the head of the German communications center in Rome. Thanks for taken care of things here, Harry. So, you decided to settle down and marry. Well, I'm happy for you."

Harry then excused himself and said he had to contact his assistant in Scotland to check out the warehouse. Bismarck was wondering what was he really up to. Then his mind began wondering about different subjects primarily about the Americans taken over his ships. Bismarck always had a sixth sense about things. He is willing to bet that Harry stands to make a sizable sum by turning those ships over to the U.S. He's probably selling them for his own profit. He will have to investigate this American take-over further.

Bismarck knows that every scam eventually runs its course and there is a time when one has to get out before the authorities come down on you. Now is the time to get out, he was convinced, but he wasn't going to say anything to Harry. He now had to find a place to invest his own profits. Switzerland again would be too risky so he decided that Argentina was the next logical place to make an investment.

With the U-boats now being destroyed at a rapid rate, the seas would be safer for transporting goods. The next profitable place to do a black-market business would be Lisbon. This was the scheme that Bismarck had talked about to Espanosa in Lisbon. Lisbon will now be his central warehouse containing all black-market goods for Europe. He decided to contact another associate, Jose Hernandez, in Argentina. He will not say a word about this new maneuver to Harry because he still did not trust him. Harry was a greedy person and would always look out for himself first. He was not to be relied on when the chips are down. Now that Bismarck is the Canadian commanding general he will have the freedom to travel to different countries and will use his position to set up his new operation.

He remained most of the day at the palace making plans for his new venture. That evening he just strolled around the Palace casino and eventually sat at the bar having a casual drink. He looked around and noticed Harry was talking to a man in the lobby. Bismarck became suspicious and walked slowly towards them making sure he was not detected. He finally was close enough to see who the stranger was. Like a lightning bolt, it hit him. He immediately recognized the stranger as the right hand man of Pietro Colombo, the Mafioso. He said to himself, "Shit! Harry's double crossing me. The bastard."

Bismarck now knows he is being set-up and by leaving the Canadian headquarters he lost his security. He thought the mob would have forgotten him by now, but they won't quit until they get their vendetta. His problem now is getting back to the safety of the base. He was wondering if Harry knew about the secret lift that he used once before in his last attempt to escape which caused John Wilson to be killed. Bismarck decided not to chance it. Mary may have told him.

Bismarck watched the lobby awhile longer and finally saw the stranger leave. They surely will be waiting for him outside. He then place a call to the Canadian headquarters. Within a half an hour there was an armored truck and five jeeps parked in front of the Palace that were loaded with Canadian soldiers. The soldiers then formed a human shield up to the Palace entrance. General Perkins casually walked out protected by the shield of these soldiers and climbed onto the armored truck. People in the casino were looking on wondering what was this military occasion all about. He was then driven away unharmed. He out-smarted the Mafia once again. Bismarck knew that there will be other attempts on his life. They will never quit. The first thing he must do, however, is eliminate Harry for being a traitor.

Bismarck contacted a hit-man he knew in the states who intern gave him the name of another hit-man in London. He then had the Canadian MPs pick up this man and bring him to his headquarters. The man's name was Preston Mulberry who was immediately ushered into the general's office. He didn't know why he was being arrested, but he didn't have a choice.

Preston stood before the general and began demanding his release. "What do you want me for? I haven't committed any crime."

"Please be seated, Mr. Mulberry. I'm General Perkins commander of the Canadian Air Corps here in England. You are not being arrested." Bismarck walked slowly behind him like he was being interrogated. "I understand that you know a Mr. Salvatore Carmillo living in New York?"

"No sir. Can't say's that I do." He lied.

"That's funny. I just had a conversation with him on a long distance phone call and he recommended you for a very important assignment that pays twenty thousand pounds. He said you're the best in Europe."

Mulberry was first startled at Bismarck's remark. Why would a general want to employ his services? He was nervous and began stuttering, "Well, Ah... come to think of it, I may have heard of him. I'm not exactly sure. What sort of an assignment are you talking about, General?"

Bismarck gave him an envelope with piece of paper in it which listed a man's name and his home address. Included in the envelope was a man's photo and the first half of his payment of 10,000 pounds in cash, that is if he accepts this assignment.

Bismarck then said, "I want the full treatment given to this individual. Do we understand each other? You will receive the rest of the money after you have completed your assignment."

Preston put the envelope in his jacket pocket and said, "I will carry out your orders, General. Give me a week's time and it shall be taken care of."

Preston was not a large man. He was only five foot six inches in height and about one hundred thirty pounds. He was now in his early forties and had served time in the big house. He was never married but had a child from a former girlfriend. Whenever he concluded a high paying contract he would send a large cashiers check to his son with no name attached to it. The boy's mother knew where it came from but she would never reveal his father's identity to the boy, especially now that she was married to another man and has two other children to take care of.

The waiting jeep took Preston back to his home. Sure enough one week later Bismarck received a phone call from Mary. She was sobbing. "Bill. Harry was killed last night in Scotland. Why would anyone want him dead." She was now crying out loud and Bismarck had a hard time consoling her.

"Mary. You must understand that we are in a risky business. There are all kinds of characters out there that want us dead. Just calm yourself. Who knows how many enemies he's acquired over the years. I can't come to you myself right now because of the war, but I will call you as often as I can. You will now have to run the business by yourself for awhile until I can find a suitable replacement for Harry." He then hung up.

That very evening Preston Mulberry was ushered back to the base. Bismarck gave him another envelope containing the balance of his payment.

"You did a fine job, Preston. How are you making out so far in England? Are you working steady?"

"Well, sir. To tell you the truth, this is the first real payoff that I've had since the war started. The only reason I'm not at the front lines is because of a wound I sustained from a copper in another assignment. They gave me two years in the big house so I'm trying to get back into business. Because of the war there aren't too many jobs in my line anymore. I had to work in the factories to make a living working on trucks. Can you imagine that, me, an accomplished professional, working in a factory for measly wages. It's down right degrading, that's what it is."

At this point Bismarck made him another offer, "How would you like to work for me making a steady thirty-grand a year and special bonuses for special favors?"

"Sounds interesting. Do I have to continue in my line of work?"

"Yes and no. First, I want you to run a warehouse of black-market goods to be sold throughout England. Your other line of business will only be required on occasions."

An so, Bismarck had a new employee to run his English racket. Now he can concentrate on the Lisbon venture. He then called his orderly and had him make arrangements for him to fly to Argentina. He left orders that Colonel Jefferies will assume command while he was away.

After he made arrangements with Hernandez in Argentina, he flew to Portugal and made contact with his counter part, Señor Espanosa, whom he met in Lisbon to discussed his new endeavor. The connections were eventually completed and a second black market ring was now established in Portugal through Argentina.

The European War Ends

On May 7, 1945, a group of German envoys signed the unconditional surrender which officially ended the European war. The war with Japan was still in progress but didn't affect Bismarck. His black-market business in England was doing better than ever. The conversion to peace time material was slow but the demand for goods in England and Europe were greater than ever. Bismarck's warehouse in Scotland was being depleted and Preston was becoming concerned. He placed a call to Bismarck at the Canadian headquarters.

"General Perkins. Our stock is getting awfully low but the demand for goods is growing. What should we do?"

"I hate to tell you this, Preston, but the racket is over. When the stock is gone you will have to close up shop. The casino will also have to be closed. The English government will no longer tolerate our existence now that the war is over. It's only a matter of time. I'm already hearing bad remarks from the English Parliament about our business. We better get out when we can and salvage whatever profits that are left. Tell Mary to close shop and to invest her shares in a legit enterprise. You both should be well off financially for the rest of your lives. I still cannot leave the base because I'm still on the Mafia's hit list in New York."

"Do you want me to handle your problem in New York for you, Bill?" asked Preston.

Bismarck at first was a little startled by his proposal, "If you could do this for me it would be worth a million American dollars."

"Say no more. It shall be done. I'll be over to get more details from you and after that I will meet with Salvatore Carmillo and together we shall take that monkey off of your back."

"I hope so, Preston. If it goes off, the million dollars will the best investment that I have ever made."

A month later a small article was written in the back pages of the London Times which read, "The head Mafioso chief of New York, Pietro Columbo, was killed while having his hair cut at a Bowery barber shop in lower Manhattan. He was gunned down gangland style with machine gun fire by two unidentified men who were wearing stockings masks over their heads."

Bismarck was elated. He decided to wait a week and then he will try his luck at leaving the base. Sure enough, a week later, he was able to walk around London with no attempts on his life and later discovered, from a few street contacts, that the contract for his life was no longer in circulation. He then paid a visit to the Palace and met with Mary and Preston.

"Preston, I want to thank you for the favor you did for me in the United States. Here is a cashiers check to cover your expenses. Will you take care of Salvatore's share for me. I have now decided to leave whatever business is left to the both of you. I have also transferred the title of the palace to you both and you can do with it whatever you wish. I'm retiring from the military and will be going back to the states, but before I do, I have to go to Italy and find Lisa. The last time I left her she was pregnant with my child. You both have enough savings that you could live the rest of your lives in comfort so you won't need me any longer."

Preston then remarked, "Before you go, Bill, I would like you to be the best man at my wedding."

"That's wonderful Preston. Who's the lucky girl? Do I know her?"

"You certainly do. It's Mary."

A little shocked Bismarck could only say, "Well! How about that." After a moment of consideration he said, "This time Mary I think you made a wise decision. I wish you both all the luck in the world."

Mary then said, "Thank you, Bill. If we have another male child we will name it Perkins Mulberry after you since you did so much for us both. That means we will have two sons named after you. Also, we have decided not to sell the Palace, but we will convert it back to a hotel. Thanks to you we now have the finances to remodel it."

"That's a great idea. Now about the child's name. I never told you what my real name is, but it's not Perkins. It is actually William Jones and my nickname is Bismarck Jones."

"You mean you are the famous Bismarck Jones?" asked Preston. "No wonder we are so successful. Your reputation is known through out Europe. I'm certainly proud to have worked with the great Bismarck. Wait till I tell my associates." Bismarck just grinned.

Mary then said, "If you don't mind, Bill, I would still like to use Perkins as the name of my second son. Jones Mulberry just doesn't seem to fit."

Bismarck beamed, "Mary, I would still be honored that you chose my alias as a name of your second son, if you have a son, that is? I'm sorry that I can't stay for the wedding, but I must be off. Adieu to both of you and if you ever need my assistance for any reason just call. Bye." He hugged Mary and kissed her on the cheek, he then reached over and shook Preston's hand and said, "You will do well, I'm sure." He walked out with only one thing on his mind.

After Salvatore was paid off by Preston he changed his way of life in New York. He was generally regarded as a poor hit-man. Most of his contracts were for five thousand dollars or less. This latest assassination was for five-hundred thousand dollars, which was more money than he had made totally as an exterminater over the last ten years.

It first became noticeable among the other Mifia gangsters when Salvatore, all of a sudden, had come into a large some of cash. He was squandering money all over the place, buying a pre-war Cadillac, expensive clothes, and moving into a Park Avenue apartment.

He had one weakness, however, that bothered him to no end. It was over his loss of a love affair he had with a former blond girlfriend. He met her as a hat check girl at Tiffany's and was crazy about her. Her name is Molly Olson. They used to date together until he had to go into hiding after being accused of killing a man's wife for pay. He was later caught and sent to jail but not for murder. The authorities could never prove he commited the assassination but they did get him for carring a concealled unlicensed weapon. While he was serving time Molly began keeping company with another hood named, Vito Morta. When he was released he was broke and couldn't afford to win her back. Now that Salvatore was in the money again he wanted her back at any cost or he would eradicate them both. He was determined but it won't be that easy.

One Saturday evening Salvatore went to a nightclub where he knew Vito and Molly were dining. He watched them from the bar and Molly happened to spot him. She mentioned it to Vito who then sent one of his henchmen over to ask him to leave. Salvatore got the message and walked out the front door. He went to his car and removed a Tommy gun and a couple of pistols from his trunk. He stood in the shadows and waited. When Vito and his crowd came out of the nightclub, Salvatore went into action and his Tommy gun began blazing. There was gun fire all over the place coming from Salvatore and return fire from Vito's men. In the end Molly, Vito, and his two bodyguards were slaughtered. Salvatore was slightly wounded and jumped into his car and took off.

Chuck Loretto, Columbo's replacement as the knew Mafia chief, was furious over this latest assassination. Vito was his first cousin so he put a contract out on Salvatore for one-hundred grand, but he wanted him alive to personally destroy him. Salvatore thought he was not detected as the hit-man, but the club doorman fingered him. In no time the mob picked Salvatore up at his Park Avenue apartment, gaged him and brought him to Loretto's mansion in Long Island.

Salvatore was stubborn and would not admit to the killing. Loretto then had his men torture him serverly. Salvatore finally admitted to the killing of Vito and in desperation to saving his life he also confessed that he was hired to kill Columbo by a Canadian. This unexpected news surprised Loretto. He then pointed his thumb down to his men and Salvatore was put out of his misery with an ice pick plunged into his chest.

As Loretto watched Salvatore slump to the ground he made a declaration to his right-hand man, "Let it be known to all Mafioso Patrons in America that the life of a Canadian by the name of William Perkins, who is now living in England, shall be terminated if he ever comes to America. The price on his head is one million dollars."

Back in Italy

Bismarck was not aware that a new contract was put out on his head under the name of William Perkins. He still had intentions of going back home to the good old U.S.A. after he finds Lisa.

Before going to Italy he first flew his Spitfire to Madrid. He went to a local bank there and made a deposit of fifty thousand dollars under the name of Lolita Gonzales. He then took a cab to the cottage where he had first met Lolita. He knocked on the door and there she was as pretty as ever.

She was shocked and could barely say, "Señor Perkins. Where did you come from. Come in, please."

"Thank you Lolita. But I can't stay long. I have to go to Italy to find my bride."

"I always knew there was another woman in your life, I could tell. Again, I want to thank you for risking your life to give us food. The rebel money you left us kept us alive for many months thereafter. I don't think we could have survived without it. I never forgot you for your generosity."

"The reason I came, Lolita, is that I want to thank you for your hospitality the only way I know so I'm presenting you with this bank book in your name."

She opened the book and was overwhelm. "But Señor Perkins, this is too much. I would have helped any man who was in trouble. It's too much."

"Lolita. I know of no other way to thank you and, believe me, I can well afford it. Now I must leave you." Bismarck bent over and kissed her passionately and left her weeping at the front door. He then refueled his Spitfire at the Madrid airport and flew directly to Milan.

Transportation in Italy at the end of the European war was virtually impossible. From the Milan airport he was able to purchase an old car that was constantly stalling. He finally was able to reach Lisa's estate but discovered she was wasn't there.

The servants have not heard from her since she left with him as his German bride. He quickly went back to the airport and flew his fighter to Monte Carlo hoping that she may have remained at the hotel where he had left her before he went to Spain. She was not there. He traveled to several Monte Carlo casinos and inquired of her whereabouts but to no avail. He was now becoming despondent. He went to the Italian Embassy and again he came to a dead end.

He went back to the airport and after filling his Spitfire with petrol he flew to Berlin. There must be a record somewhere of her whereabouts. He went to the German headquarters in search of any clues that might lead him to his beloved. He was told that if there were any records at all of her existence as a German prisoner he might find them in a record room where Hitler was living in his underground shelter. Hitler preferred to keep the records of all prisoners, personally. No one knew why he required them or what he would use them for. Bismarck went there but the entrance was heavily guarded by Russian soldiers. He was not allowed to enter even though he was an Allied general. He was now becoming agitated. Bismarck began yelling at the soldiers and one leveled his rifle and aimed it at him. Bismarck got the message. He then went to the Russian headquarters and asked to see the Russian general in charge. After four hours of waiting he finally was allowed to see him.

"Welcome, comrade." said the general through his interpreter. "Before we begin any discussions we must have a toast to our winning the war."

Bismarck was getting impatient but he did accept the toast. The only problem was one drink of Vodka led to another. Bismarck was still trying to get his permission to look over the records in Hitler's personal library but he was slowly becoming inebriated himself.

Finally, he was given a letter by the Russian general to allow him entrance to Hitler's bomb shelter. Bismarck then went down deep in the dungeon and came across a room where there were many file cabinets. Fortunately, they were in alphabetical order so he began looking under Marabito. Nothing. Then he looked under Countess Lisa. Again, nothing. He looked under Perkins.

Nothing, nothing! He was becoming frustrated. He was running out of names to look under. He felt defeated. Bismarck sat down trying to calm his futility. Then it came to him. When he left her she was married to a Major William von Bourn. He jumped up immediately and began looking under V. There it was, plain as day. Inside a folder was a paper covering the Major's military history and his two wives. It read:

"Major von Bourn is missing and is presumed dead. The major was married to Anna but, for some reason, he married again to a Countess Lisa Marabito, who was captured by Mussolini's blackguards. They believe there was a second von Bourn who was an imposter and together they became enemy agents for the Allies. The imposter escaped but the contessa and her son were transported by the Italian government to a prison camp in 1944 to Bizerte, Tunisia and are to remain there for the duration of the war." There was nothing else in the file.

Bismarck's yelled out loud, "I have a son."

Without hesitation he ran up the stairs as fast as he could, took a cab to the airport, and flew his plane to the city of Tunis in Africa. There he rented an auto and drove it to the city of Bizerte. He immediately went to the police station. They told him that there used to be an old Italian prisoner of war camp thirty kilometers out of town but the camp is now run by the French Government and only contain Axis prisoners. The man in charge also said that he doubted that his wife and child were there and if they were it's unlikely that they were still alive, especially if they were detained over the past three years. The death rate in that camp was very high. Bismarck hopes were still high because Lisa and his son could only have been there a year. He drove south on a dirt road to the camp.

When he arrived he saw that there were still many prisoners still mauling around in the camp. He drove up to the main gate and in French he told the guards he was General Perkins and wanted to speak with the man in charge. He was told to leave his vehicle outside of the camp and he would be escorted in. Bismarck was also told to leave his weapons in his car.

Behind a mahogany desk sitting in a very comfortable leather chair was a French officer. He was unshaven and not very presentable. It was terribly hot that summer and the officer didn't wear a coat or, for that matter, a shirt. He was in a filthy T-shirt that hadn't been washed for some time. He was drinking from a large glass that was half full of red wine.

"Ah. You are General Perkins. I'm pleased to make your acquaintance. I am Colonel Richard. Would you care for some good French wine?" Bismarck could hardly stand just looking at this crude character.

When Bismarck said no the Colonel simply shrugged his shoulders. "In that case, what can I do for you?"

"I'm looking for my wife and child. Her name is Countess Lisa Marabito, possibly better known as Mrs. von Bourn."

"There must be some mistake here, Monsieur. Mrs. von Bourn was married to a German Major. She is now considered a prisoner of war and will be tried as a spy because she was sympathetic to the German cause."

"Listen. I'm Major von Bourn. I was a spy for the English and was masqueraded as Major von Bourn. Countessa Lisa was a member of the Italian Partisans. The Partisans had asked me to impersonate the major in Rome and it would be more convincing to the German high commanders if I married the Countessa."

"Then what happened to the real major."

"I had already killed him. I was shot down over Italy in my fighter and to save myself I impersonated this major. I was very good at it because my German happens to be excellent.

"I'm sorry General. I will need more proof than just your word before I can release the countessa and her son. You see she is scheduled to appear before the magistrate tomorrow morning for her crimes and she will probably be shot that very afternoon if she is found guilty, which is expected."

"What. Are you crazy. I tell you she is my wife and she is not a German spy. I want to speak with the magistrate if you please."

"I'm sorry. That's impossible. He cannot be disturbed. There is nothing that can be done today. You may plead your case tomorrow but I assure you she is as good as dead. It's the spoils of war." The Colonel had a smirk on his face that annoyed Bismarck.

"Bull-shit. We will see about that." He was madder than hell.

Bismarck then stormed out of his office and ran to his auto. He drove into town and discovered that there was a regiment of Canadian troops camped outside of the city waiting to be transferred back to Canada. He drove to the camp and told his predicament to the commanding officer who immediately called general quarters.

Two hundred troops in trucks and three tanks headed for the prison of war camp. Bismarck was in the lead jeep. He finally stopped the caravan at the front entrance of the camp and told the French guard that he wanted to speak again with the Colonel. Colonel Richard came out to the main gate and saw this whole army ready for war.

Frustrated the Colonel said, "General. I cannot give up the countessa. You have no right to threaten me like this."

With that, Bismarck gave an order and the troops climbed out of their trucks fixing their mortar cannons and machine guns. The tanks turned into a position facing the barbed wire with their guns aiming at the main barracks.

"I will ask you once again, Colonel. Will you release the Countessa." Bismarck was now in his field. He had the cards and he knew how to bluff. But the Frenchman was stubborn and still refused.

"Fire one," was Bismarck's first command. The first tank fired a cannon shot at the Colonel's shack destroying it completely killing his personal guards and his secretary.

Bismarck was ready to give his second order when the Colonel yelled, "Stop. You must be mad. I will give her to you." He gave orders to a guard to release the Countessa and her son. A few minutes later a haggard woman came out of a barrack carring a small toddler. They both looked under nourished and she could hardly walk. Bismarck could not believe his eyes.

She held her head down and could not look at him. As he tried to greet them he said to her, "What have they done to you, my love?" He then addressed the Colonel and said, "Colonel. If anything seriously has happened to my wife and child I will hold you directly responsible. You had better pray to god that they can be restored to normal health again."

Lisa and her boy climbed into the back of the jeep with the assistance of a soldier. She continued to keep her head down and wouldn't even look at Bismarck because she was so ashamed of her appearance and her poor health. They drove back to the camp and Lisa and her son were immediately put to bed in the camp hospital.

It was almost a week before Lisa would allow Bismarck to visit with her. She couldn't bear to be seen in such poor health. She finally felt strong enough after having a steady diet of food and orange juice to allow him to visit her. But the first words she said to Bismarck was that she can no longer be his wife.

He was shocked. "What! Why not?"

"Please. Don't ask me why. I can no longer be married to you. I'm sorry, but that's the way it will have to be."

Bismarck began pleading, "Lisa. Please don't make any harsh decisions just yet. Get well first. Then we will have a long talk."

"It's no use. I have already made up my mind. I'm grateful to you for saving our lives, but after the treatment I've had in this camp I do not wish to be involved with any man. Please forgive me and let me rest. I don't wish to see you again, ever." She began to sob and asked him to leave.

Bismarck was not satisfied. He had to know more of what happened in that camp and what they did to Lisa. He had heard from the local police about another woman who had escaped from that camp and was now living in Palermo, Sicily. He flew his plane to Palermo and paid her a visit. The girl's name was Stella Lombardo.

In Italian Bismarck asked her what went on in that prison of war camp and did she know anything about the brutality that Countessa Lisa went through.

"Si, Signore. I will tell you everything. Before the Countessa arrived I was the steady girl for the colonel. He abused and raped me continuously. He would make me do things that I cannot describe to you. It was horrible. When the Countessa arrived she became his new number-one playmate. I was no longer in his favor so he let the guards have me. I was repeatedly gang raped by all of the guards. This went on for months until one of the guards foolishly fell in love with me. He was an idiot, but through him I was able to escape. I heard later that he was shot for aiding me.

"As far as the Countessa is concerned, she simply took my place as the Colonel's girl. From what I understand he was even more brutal with her than he was with me. Then one day the Countessa managed to stab him with a letter opener but, unfortunately, he survived. She was then thrown to the wolves and all of the guards used her as they did me. To hide his crimes the Colonel was going to have her shot by a firing squared as soon as a proper magistrate from France became available to make it legal. You came just in time to save her life. That is all I know of what had happened to her, Signore.

"Thank you very much for your frankness. Now I know why the Countessa doesn't want anything to do with me. She feels that she has been ruined and is no longer worthy of me because of what happened in that concentration camp," he had trouble containing his anger.

Bismarck flew back to Tunis and drove back to the Canadian camp. He mustered his troops once again and headed back to the prison camp that very night. They set up their positions as they did before and when Bismarck gave the orders the guards at the front gate were immediately shot to death with machine gun fire. Two-hundred Canadian troops then entered the camp killing arbitrarily any French guard they came across. Bismarck lead the attack and he headed directly to the Colonel's new quarters. Two Canadian soldiers broke his door down and the Colonel was caught laying in bed naked with a female prisoner.

"What is the meaning of this, General." The gun shots didn't originally disturb him because it was common in that camp. His soldiers were always shooting disobedient prisoners. He thought nothing of it.

Bismarck shouted to the girl to get dressed and get out. He then turned his pistol toward the Colonel and said, "This is for what you did to my Lisa."

He first shot him in the left leg, then the right arm. "You pig. You raped my wife."

"Please General. I can explain." He was bleeding and

begging for mercy.

Bismarck then aimed his gun to the Colonel's lower body and proceeded to shoot off his testicles. The Colonel was screaming with pain. Bismarck waited awhile. He wanted the Colonel to suffer a little longer. He finally raised his gun and shot him in the head. He then gave orders to his men, "Take no French prisoners!"

With that order every guard in the camp was killed and all the war prisoners were set free. It was a massive exodus of one thousand war prisoners, both male and female, running out the gate and in many different directions. When all was clear Bismarck gave the orders to burn the place down. "I want no evidence!" There was an investigation later but no one could determine who did the killings. The French authorities concluded that it was due to a local uprising of Tunisian rebels and dropped the investigation.

Bismarck then went back to the hospital to visit with Lisa. She at first refused to see him but he was persistent. He looked at her with pity. But now he felt better. He had his revenge.

"By the way. That prison of war camp you were in no longer exists. I have killed all of the guards who have harmed you and I personally killed the Colonel myself. I accomplished my vendetta for you, my love. You will never be abused by anyone again." He was firm with his explanation.

She look up at him and repeated her position, "It doesn't make any difference, William. I am a ruined woman. Don't you understand? I would no longer make you a suitable wife. It would be a burden on your shoulders for the rest of my life. You will always resent me."

Bismarck then tried to contain his anger and said, "My dear. Don't talk now. Just rest. Next week I will take you and my son, William Junior, back to the United States and we will lick this thing, together. Time has a way of healing all things. I still love you my dear and nothing is going to change that."

Lisa could see that he was determined and replied, "William, please be patient with me. I need time. Time alone. Please take me back to my home in Milan and let me and little William rest there. Go back to New York and settle your affairs. Give me at least six months to recuperate. By then, I will know for sure if I still want a life with you. Please, William. I'm begging you."

"All right, Lisa. I will do as you wish," and they embraced. Tears were now running down her cheek and she began to feel little better. She needs that time to get her life back. When she was in better health they all flew to Milan. Bismarck didn't even enter her home. He said his goodbyes but did not go directly to New York. He first flew to Venice. He had one last bit of business to attend to that concerned a certain Count Marco Del Monte.

Back in New York

After Bismarck left Venice he flew back to England. He then submitted his resignation and a week later he was officially discharged from the Canadian Air Corps. He paid Mary and Preston one more visit and then left for America.

He landed in Laguardia airport in New York, and as he was heading for the luggage area he recognized a man talking to an attendant. Bismarck carefully hid himself behind a column but close enough to hear their conversation.

The man said, "His name is Perkins. He was supposed to arrive here on this flight. It is essential that I speak with him."

"I'm sorry sir. I can't help you. You might try holding up a sign or have his name announced on the loud speaker system."

The man then went over to a flight hostess who just came through the exit door from the plane. He asked her if she knew if there was a Mr. Perkins on board. She said he already had left. The man immediately waved to several hoods standing by and they all ran towards the baggage department.

Bismarck surmised that it was the Mafia still after him but now they are looking for a Mr. Perkins. Since he was not recognized when he first entered the waiting room he decided that they were not looking for a Mr. Jones. Instead of retrieving his luggage he went directly out into the street, hailed a cab and told the driver to take him to Babylon, Long Island.

In his small home in Babylon he made several phone calls. All of his reliable contacts said basically the same thing. The hit contract that is out is only for a William Perkins. There was no mention of an William Jones. Bismarck was greatly relieved for this information but wondered who had squealed on him. He then made a call to Preston Mulberry in England.

"Preston. What's going on here? There is a contract out for Perkins but not for Jones. Do you know anything about it?"

"No, I don't, Bill. But I will surely find out. Give me your number and I'll call you back."

Bismarck waited for three hours and finally his phone rang.

"Bill," said Preston. "It was Salvatore. He spilled the beans on you before they killed him, but he only referred to you as William Perkins. As Jones you are in the clear since only Mary and I know your true alias."

"Thank you Preston. Your a great friend," and rang off the receiver.

A gruesome thought entered his mind. If he was to do away with Mary and Preston, no one else in America could identify him as Perkins. He decided that wasn't the way. They were his only true and trusted friends left. He was sure that the mob will stay away from England now that the war is over. The English laws will become strict again and any mobsters would immediately be picked up as they entered the country.

On another day, when he was at a super market in Long Island, he spotted a man that he thought he recognized. He couldn't place the face at first but he was sure he had met him before. As he was unpacking his groceries at his home it struck him. It was that old golfer whom he took twenty thousand bucks from on the golf course many years ago. "What was his name.... Nichols. That's it. Steven Nichols. The sun-of-a bitch had spotted me. Damn! If it's not the Mafia after me it's one of my old conquests. Shit!"

Bismarck went home and opened up a safe which he had hidden in the basement of his Long Island home and removed two pistols. He figured Nichols will now be gunning for him personally himself especially since all of his other attempts to destroy him have failed. He was tired of running and has now decided to have a showdown with Nichols once and for all, right here in Long Island if necessary.

A funny thing then happened. A telegram was delivered to him at his front door. This puzzled Bismarck since none of his friends knew he was here. He opened the gram and it said, "For one million big ones, at Beth Page Country club, lefty or righty, tomorrow morning at ten. I want eight strokes." It was initialed S.N.

Bismarck grinned to himself. "The bastard is challenging me for one last round of golf. Hell, I haven't played in years. If I win he'll have me killed anyway. But if I lose... I wonder."

The next morning Bismarck showed up at the country club which was only a few miles away. He had to rent a set of golf clubs and then waited at the bar. Ten minutes later Mr. Nichols walked in with two tough looking guys tagging along. Bismarck assumed they were his enforces. Nichols walked right up to him and sat on the stool next to him and said, "Fine day for golf, wouldn't you say?"

"It sure is a nice day to make money," replied Bismarck.

"You have been very allusive, Mr. Jones. Now I want my revenge. Do you agree with my terms?"

"I'm not sure. I want you to know that I haven't played for years so I'm a bit rusty. How about making it five strokes?"

"Very well, your on. First, I want to make a toast you, Bismarck, for all of your ventures. You made a lot of people poor with your gambling and rackets, but now your empire is about to be destroyed, one way or another."

Under his breath Bismarck simple said, "Shit." He knew what he meant when he said, "one way or another." They toasted together with a shot of rye whiskey and quickly downed their drinks. Two cashiers checks were written ahead of time payable to the other person. Bismarck had known the procedure and previously went to his bank the day before. The checks were given to the bartender to hold. The winner of the match would simply rip up his own check and cash the other one. The bartender was amazed at the amount of money in the checks and put them in a safe under the counter. They both headed for the first tee.

Whenever Bismarck was involved in a sting operation he would always make sure he would come out on top. This time, however, he was not so sure. It has been awhile since he played. They flipped a coin to see who goes first and Nichols won. The game was on. Bismarck noticed that Nichols's henchmen were walking towards the seventeenth hole. He knew then that the assassination will take place there. It was far removed from the club house and isolated. Bismarck had his guns hidden in his golf bag and will remove them before they reach the seventeenth hole no matter what the score is.

Bismarck was definitely rusty and was have a tough time

keeping up with Nichols. It was obvious that Nichols was still playing several times a week. Even though Nichols was now several years older, Bismarck noticed he played more conservatively and didn't take unnecessary chances as he did the last time they played. By the tenth hole Nichols was two strokes ahead. Bismarck was gaining but it wasn't easy for him.

Now that they were coming to the seventeenth tee the score was tied. Bismarck knew that if he lost to Nichols he would most likely be spared, but he was having troubles with that. It was not the money or his life that was at stake here, it was winning the game. Intentionally losing was against all of the principles that he had stood for. It was an obsession with him. He had to win at any cost. Nichols could see Bismarck was now nervous as he watched him wipe the sweat off of his forehead. Nichols just grinned to himself as he knew the strain that Bismarck was going through. He knew him like a book and was aware that Bismarck couldn't stand the though of being defeated intentionally or otherwise.

Nichols grinned and said to himself, "Will he deliberately lose to me to save his life or would he rather die a winner. In either case I will be the winner." He could see his men in the distance waiting near the seventeenth hole to finish Bisamrck off if necessary.

The seventeenth hole was a 450 yard par four. It was to Bismarck's advantage because he could easily out-drive Nichols by fifty yards. Sure enough he drove 280 yards and Nichols could only drive 230 yards. This left Bismarck with 170 yards to the green but Nichols had 220 yards to go which was beyond his capability from the fareway. Nichols second shot was slightly off to the right about twenty yards short of the green, but Bismarck was on the green and only five feet away from the pin.

As they approached the green the two henchman appeared out of nowhere on each side of the green just standing there waiting for Nichols's signal. Bismarck went to his bag as though he wanted to remove his putter but instead he took out two 45 caliber pistols. Without hesitation, he began blasting away at the two men killing them both. He then swirled himself around and hit the ground while firing at Nichols's caddie whose gun was also out but he never got the chance to use it. Bismarck then aimed his guns at Nichols.

"Make your next golf shot!" he commanded. Nichols was dumbfounded. He was so nervous he dubbed his shot and his ball went into a bunker. He took two strokes to get out of the bunker and finally ended up with a seven on that hole. Bismarck birdied the hole and was now four strokes ahead. Bismarck's caddie was stunned watching the whole event but he didn't say a word. He couldn't.

"I concede, Bismarck. There is no sense playing any further." Bismarck acknowledge Nichols's plea by droping his putter but continued aiming his gun at him.

They both walked back to the clubhouse together. As they entered Bismarck's gun was against Nichols back who was careful not to agitate him for any reason and followed his every order. Nichols told the bartender he lost the game and to give the checks to Bismarck. They then proceeded to the parking lot still close together and stopped at Nichols's car. Nichols had already resolved to his fate. He knew he was a dead duck and could only hope that Bismarck would have a little sympathy. He was told to get into his Caddy.

As Nichols sat behind the steering wheel Bismarck said, "Mr. Nichols, consider yourself lucky. I'm not going to kill you this time. You see, I was completely thrilled with the game and all the pressure you provided. It was the most exciting time that I have ever had. The odds were very much against me in every respect but, as you obviously know, I loved the competition and the challenge you furnished was outstanding. You made my day, Mr. Nichols, so I'm letting you go free. However, the next time we meet I may not be so generous. Good day Mr. Nichols, and thanks for a wonderful game and of cause, the money." Nichols was relieved. He couldn't believe he was still alive. Bismarck simply walked away. Nichols just sat there flabbergasted.

Bismarck first went back to the club house and gave his own caddie twenty thousand dollars in cash and told him to keep his mouth shut or he may receive the same treatment that the other caddies receive. When Bismarck drove out into the street he could hear sirens from police cars approaching the golf course.

Bismarck took his time and slowly drove right past Nichols and waved at him as he drove away.

Nichols was still in his car watching the whole affair. He was visably shaking. He finally composed himself and as he watched Bismarck exit the course he said, "What a magnificent Con artist. He is truly the greatest Wheeler-Dealer of all time." His praise for Bismarck was genuine and he was still grateful to be alive. That was a close call he thought, but he knew there will be another encounter. This latest confrontation will not stop Nichols because he also enjoys a challenge. He'll begin working on another attempt at destroying Bismarck as soon as he goes home. The next time he'll be more careful, he thought.

Now that Bismarck was sure he was free from all his enemies he sent a telegram to Lisa. "I'm coming to Milan whether you are ready for me or not. I cannot wait any longer for your answer. You had better make arrangements at a church for our wedding because we are going to be married like it or not. Love, William." He didn't care about the bad ordeal she went through. He desided to be intense because he couldn't stand to live without her.

When he arrived at her home in Milan, she greeted him with open arms and was crying. He kissed her furiously and it seemed that her dilemma was over. After a moment when things settled down they began talking about different subjects and especially about how she got over her depression. She had to admit that his telegram was so forceful she couldn't refuse him any longer.

Then out of the blue she said, "By the way, William. You know that cousin of mine who had raped me when I was young. Well, would you believe it, he was assassinated. He was found dead with his privates in his mouth. The authorities think it was the Mafia because that's the technique they usually use as a warning to others. At least now I won't receive any more of those nasty phone calls."

"Isn't that something," remarked Bismarck. "He must have offended someone in the Mafia pretty badly for him to be killed in such a fashion like that." Bismarck had a funny grin on his face and Lisa had her suspicions, but she would never question him about it.

When Bismarck initially went to see the Count at his estate that morning he found it well guarded. Fortunately, there were no guard dogs present so Bismarck scaled the wall and entered the mansion through a window. He went upstairs and glimpsed into each room and finally found the Count asleep in one of the bedrooms. Bismarck, by now, was not satisfied with just killing this man. His contempt for him was so overwhelming he had to resort to torture. He wanted to make sure the Count knew why he was being punished and ultimately killed.

Bismarck first rendended him unconscious with a blow to the head with a black jack. He then gagged him and tied him to a chair. When the Count revived Bismarck introduced himself and explained why he was there. He went over with him about all of the gruesome details of his raping Lisa and continued to hound her. Now it was his turn to pay for his past deeds. Bismarck, at first, intended to use his knife on him and watch him suffer and bleed to death, but that makeup was not in his character so, in the end, he decided to just do away with him as quickly as possible. He finished him off with his knife and proceeded to complete the ritual in such a fashion to implicate the Mafia as the culprit. He then left the crime scene the same way he came in.

Lisa and Bismarck were married a week after he arrived. This time the ceremony was properly done with many Italians cheering the Countessa's marriage to the rich Americano. Bismarck paid all the leans that were against Lisa's property and her noble heritage in Milan was restored. Their son was given the title of Count William Maribito Jones. Even Preston and Mary came down from England to attend the wedding.

Bismarck decided it would be safer to raise his family in Italy for awhile rather than taking the risk of living in the United States. Who knows, someone might connect the name of Perkins as being the great Bismarck Jones. Even if they did make the connection he would give ten to one odds that they would never be able to get to him. He was that conceited. He was truly the greatest hustler and confidence man that had ever lived. His only weakness was that he couldn't stay away from the challenge of a game. He knew in his heart that he could never completely retire from the gambling competition even in Italy. After all, Milan is only 200 miles from Monaco.

The End

About the Author

Joseph Francis Panicello was born in Queens, New York, in 1927. He was married for thirty years to his late wife, Rose, and is now residing with Barbara Coulter for the past nine years. He has three daughters and seven grandchildren.

Mr. Panicellos is a World War II veteran. He has used his navy experiences to write his first book, *Vindicated*, and has incorporated his aerospace experience to write his second book, *Brian's Comet.*

Prior to pursuing his writing career, the author maintained a successful 40 year career as an electronic engineer for Lockheed Aerospace in Burbank, California and Bell Telephone Laboratories in Whippany, New Jersey.

Mr. Panicello has already completed seven manuscripts and two have been published. He is a member of the American Fiction Society and the National Writers Association.